RISING EAST: *The Journal of East London Studies*

Volume One *Number Three*

Rising East: The Journal of East London Studies is published three times a year by Lawrence & Wishart on behalf of the University of East London. The university acknowledges the generous contribution of the London East Training and Enterprise Council (LETEC) in co-funding this journal.

Design and Setting Art Services, Norwich
Marketing consultant, Jonathan Keane

Subscriptions

For 1998, subscription rates are:

UK:	Individuals £20,	Institutions £50,
	Corporate Subscribers £100,	
Rest of the world:	Individuals £30,	Institutions £60,
	Corporate Subscribers £110.	

Single copies £10

All subscriptions administered by:

Lawrence & Wishart
99a Wallis Road, London E9 5LN
Tel: 0181 533 2506
Fax: 0181 533 7369

Contributions, correspondence and books for review

Send to: Tim Butler, Editor, *Rising East: The Journal of East London Studies*, Department of Sociology, University of East London, Longbridge Road, Dagenham RM8 2AS.

Prospective writers are encouraged to contact the editors to discuss their ideas and to obtain a copy of our style sheet.

ISSN 1367 787X
ISBN 085315 870 3

Printed in Great Britain by Cambridge University Press, Cambridge

The Feature articles in Rising East *are refereed by experts in the relevant field before being accepted for publication.*

Contents

Volume 1: Issue 3

Notes on Contributors

Tim Butler is Principal Lecturer in Sociology at the University of East London. He co-edited with Mike Rustin, *Rising in the East? The regeneration of East London* (1996) and is author of *Gentrification and the Middle Classes* (1997).

Phil Cohen is Reader in Cultural Studies at the University of East London where he directs the Centre for New Ethnicities Research. His most recent publications are *Rethinking the Youth Question* (1997) and *Island Stories* (1997).

John Eade is Reader in Sociology and Anthropology at the Roehampton Institute, London. He is author of *The Politics of Community: the Bangladeshi community in East London*. He recently edited a book entitled *Living the Global City: globalisation as local process.*

Chris Mele is Assistant Professor in the Department of Sociology at the State University of New York at Buffalo, USA. He has written on East Village in *From Urban Village to East Village: the battle for New York's Lower East Side* (1994).

Martin Simmons and **Abigail Warren** work for the London Planning Advisory Committee to which Martin Simmons is chief planner and Abigail Warren a senior planner.

Stephen Timms is Labour MP for East Ham.

David Dundon-Smith works at London East TEC where he is the Economic and Business Analyst. The *Trends East* article was put together by a team which includes Roger Morfey, Seamus Newe and Darren Simmonds.

Andrew Attfield is seconded from the London Borough of Hackney to carry out the role of Project Programme Manager for Dalston City Partnership. He has been working on the Shoreditch developments for the past five years.

Elizabeth Greenhalgh has been working in urban and cultural policy for the last ten years.

Cathy Ross is Head of the Department of Later London History at the Museum of London. Recent projects have incldued 'London Now', the museum's new post-war gallery, opened in January 1997. She has a particualr interset in Bethnal Green.

Nana Yaa Mensah is a journalist, editor and radio broadcaster with a particular iterest in Africa. Currently she works for *West Africa* magazine, and in 1995 organised the literature programme for *Africa 95*.

Reform versus Regeneration

IN THE EDITORIAL TO THE FIRST ISSUE, I invited (more in hope than anticipation, it has to be said) comments on the journal and offers to write for it. I have been pleasantly surprised by the offers to write for it - on the gay scene in Tower Hamlets, on the flora and fauna of East London and on the cultural industries in Hackney to name but three. I have had several comments, mostly complimentary, often from people who thought they were going to have to be polite but were, as it turned out, genuinely able to say how much they had enjoyed reading it - particularly the *Trends East* and *Artyfacts* sections. I have only had one written comment (from my colleague Paul Watt) who raised a number of issues, one of which is worth quoting at length:

> It's interesting that although much of the editorial and the first two articles talk a lot about regeneration (mainly at this regional/sub regional level) there seems to be scant recognition of the fact that East London has *already* been a key site for most of the urban regeneration strategies of the last fifty years. And what have been the results, and what conclusions can we draw from this? My own, rather predictable, response would be to argue that there is a world of difference between 'regeneration' (providing more jobs, better services, etc.) and major economic and social structural reform. Without the latter, the deep structural inequalities which have so characterised London for a very long time, will simply remain, albeit in new guises.

He's right: this issue of contexualising regeneration and the distinction between regeneration and structural reform is key. If I needed any further convincing, it came coincidentally as I started to write this editorial in a review by Sue Brownill of a collection I edited with Michael Rustin *Rising in the East? The Regeneration of East London* (Butler and Rustin 1996). Whilst generally supportive of the book, she says:

> ...the whole notion of 'regeneration' is widely recognized as being open to competing definitions and interpretations. This is not addressed in the introduction, nor do the editors reveal which view of regeneration they subscribe to. Important points - for example, from David Albury and Carole Snee, who state in their chapter on higher education that 'regeneration is a process shaped by coalitions and alliances, a struggle for competing visions of communities and futures (p366) - demand attention across the range of contributions. East London itself has been the site of competing visions of regeneration for many decades and would have provided fertile ground for a greater investigation of their meaning, implications and relative successes and failures.

This is fair comment and, coming with that from Paul Watt, needs some sort of answer. The longer answer is that we needed a new government (which we now have) and some new thinking (which hopefully is being done - not least in this journal) and perhaps another book. In the shorter term we need to be clearer about what we mean and where we stand. This university, from its inception as the North East London Polytechnic in the early 1970s, set out the principles on which it operated - which were broadly regeneration-oriented. Of those principles, the one which sticks in my mind is the criteria of 'likely to benefit' which enjoined admissions tutors to go out of their way to offer places to local people who might benefit from the course at the expense, if necessary, of better qualified traditional school-leavers. This was at a time in the early 1970s when such 'gatekeepers' were meant to allow in only those with five 'O' levels and two good 'A' levels. The University has managed to build on this and to develop the kind of strategy developed by Albury and Snee, both of whom are editorial board members of this journal, to get the resources for a major new campus in the Royal Docks from the Single Regeneration Budget in partnership with a number of other organisations. Such partnerships impose their own restraints which was probably what the Government intended: nothing was to be of right, everything had to be the subject of a bid. Getting *any* additional resources for East London over and above the minimal levels contained in departmental budgets has involved setting up partnerships with all sorts of organisations for all sorts of projects which might not be the first ones that one would identify as necessary for regeneration (better services and more jobs), let alone for serious structural social and economic reform. However all that is now behind us, and ironically, one legacy of the Tory years is a sense of a sub region and an understanding of the need to work together and to have to think through the case for what is required. Hopefully the New Labour government will now build on this creatively.

But is it regeneration or structural reform? This is similar to the question posed by the Marxist left between reform and revolution; the usual answer to which is that revolutionaries always back reform in the sure knowledge that capitalism cannot deliver the goods whereupon the workers, realising the limitations of capitalism, opt for revolution. If pigs had wings. Capitalism has shown itself very good at offering just enough reform to keep sufficient people on board at any one period in time - if the workers are busy papering the parlour then they have no time to bother about revolution. Marxism turns out to have been a rather better analyst of capitalism than architect for socialism.

So this journal, as I argued in the first issue, is about giving a voice to the sub region and, as Michael Rustin has suggested in the second issue, it is not about creating a plan but encouraging a conversation between many of the different actors involved from which, hopefully, will emerge a strategy and a series of initiatives designed to achieve that strategy. I doubt if there will ever be an endpoint and would be very surprised if, in fifty years time, one could claim that East London had been 'regenerated'. It is likely, given these constraints and differences, that there will be tensions within the journal between - for sake of argument - the kinds of articles by Whyatt and Stevenson (in issue 1) and Timms (this issue), and those by Home (issue 1) and Cohen (this issue). It is inevitable that some form of sub-regional boosterism will emerge but hopefully that will be more than balanced by the (constructively) critical approach which is the hallmark of good university research.

We do need to return to the issue of what is meant by East London. The rumours - hopefully unfounded - have been doing the rounds that the Government does not see London as a priority for regeneration. This would be a mistake and is why we have concerned ourselves with identifying an area based on the Thames Gateway, north and south of the river east from Tower Bridge which we have termed a sub region. This implies a significant part of the London regional economy and one whose needs are as great as any other area of the United Kingdom but which cannot at the same time be understood, except as part of the London economy. It is unfortunately a fact of life that just as wealth creates poverty, so rich areas create poor areas and without state intervention they will remain pauperised. East London has for the last one hundred years been regarded as a touchstone for larger and wider social processes and, unusually, has been chronicled by social scientists - Charles Booth, and Willmott and Young spring to mind - in ways that reached (and touched) a wider audience and which led directly (or indirectly) to some of the most significant social welfare reforms of the twentieth century. We should not therefore be too surprised that when *Panorama* were searching around for a peg on which to hang a programme about blaming educational failure on mothers, they alighted on some research being undertaken by an editorial board member of this journal in Dagenham which, as readers will know, made no such claims. In essence, what East London manages to summon up, at any given period of time, is the state of class relations in Britain which are always much more complex, convoluted and contradictory than either class warriors or their postmodern critics might wish us to believe. East London, taken as a whole, has never been a working-class area in the sense that a majority of its inhabitants have constituted an industrial working class. East London in the twentieth century has been a microcosm of the class accommodations that make up capitalism and always have done. One hundred years ago the cheerleaders of the middle class were as enthusiastic as those of Karl Marx's daughter Eleanor when the dockers went on strike, because it symbolised that the people of East London were, at long last, behaving as the working class should, that is as a disciplined group led by those favouring - depending on your view point - reform or revolution. The issue, then as now, was that of social exclusion and, for the next three quarters of a century, governments found methods of incorporating the population of East London into the economic mainstream until Mrs Thatcher succeeded where the Luftwaffe failed. In this sense then, the history of regeneration in East London is at least one hundred years old. Arguably, what it achieved is a degree of social quiescence often at the cost of intolerable intolerance towards fellow citizens. What, without doubt, it has not achieved is any significant permanent restructuring of social and economic relations: East London remains London's poorest quarter but at the same time a remarkably diffuse and vibrant place. The danger, however, is that forces of globalisation will now make it into a ghetto from which no hope will ever emerge. There are few, if any, 'no go areas' in London of the sort which characterise cities the length of the Americas; unless 'something is done' there is a real danger that this will happen. When London's middle-class citizens begin to fear parts of their own city, like their counterparts in New York City, Mexico City or Rio then it will be too late. It may, of course, be that whilst there are no such 'no go areas', many of London's middle class avoid East London simply because there is nothing of interest to them there - if so, this tells us a lot about contemporary middle-class culture(s).

Social exclusion, however, like its cousin social polarisation, is an infuriating term and tells us little - all hitherto existing societies have excluded significant parts of their population. It is not necessary to be a Marxist to argue that the majority of the population, despite the acquisition of formal rights of social and political citizenship, are excluded from power and decision-making. With the globalisation of capitalism, ordinary men and women, as well as nation-states probably have less control than ever before. What has undoubtedly changed over the last century is the complexity of the inclusion/ exclusion relation: issues of gender, ethnicity, place and sexuality have now joined those of class as talked-about dimensions of belonging-not belonging. Exclusion is, then, essentially a political term describing those who, for one reason or another, do not feel that they have a 'stake' in the society and, as it was a hundred years ago, the main arbiter of this is full-time employment. It is not, however, necessary to develop a coherent theoretical account of social exclusion in order to understand the problem. Peter Mandelson in his lecture to the Fabian Society defined it as people feeling that they do not have a say about what goes on and therefore feel that they have no responsibility for doing anything about their situation. It is not just about poverty or unemployment, it is about *feeling* socially and politically ignored which needs to be addressed. After nearly two decades of a government that went out of its way to rub people's noses in their own unimportance, it is very encouraging to hear senior government ministers say that they care about the inclusion of people in politics. It is not unrelated to the feelings that were aroused by, and expressed in reaction to, the death of Diana, Princess of Wales amongst many ordinary people, but especially women and ethnic minorities. People identified with her as *their* princess precisely because she did not see them as subjects but as people.

When we talk about regeneration it is this feeling of marginalisation and disposability that we have to focus on. It is about dealing with the tendency of capitalism to marginalise those on the edge of the social system as the price for maintaining the economic system. It now looks increasingly unlikely that the gravediggers of capitalism will ever be its own working class as Marx predicted but, rather will be those who, through their own choice or lack of choice, are outside the mainstream of 'the system' which can be defined as the capital-labour relationship. Thirty years ago sociologists were interested in why people revolted - the problem was interesting in the sense that it either involved history (the sans culottes of the French Revolution) or those living in far-off countries. The assumption was that we, in what were then termed the 'advanced industrial nations', had cracked the problem through welfare statist social policies and Keynesian demand management. These sociologists came to the conclusion that there was what they termed a 'J Curve' effect, much as the French sociologist Durkheim had shown in the case of suicide: when people were so poor that they had to concentrate on survival, they had no appetite for revolution (or suicide); this only occurred when their rising expectations were not matched by a rise in what was termed their 'capabilities', their material circumstances. The success, if you can call it that, of the last twenty years has been to have brought the 'third world' home to London and to have left the people with so little hope that they have made so few demands of the political system. It was unimaginable to Clive Jenkins writing twenty years ago that you could have upwards of two million unemployed people and maintain social and political order (Jenkins and Sherman 1979). Whilst it might have made sense in the 1930s to have dealt with exclusion from work and civil society by having people dig holes and fill them in or, more sensibly, by building autobahns, damming rivers to create cheap electricity and building electricity grids, this is not what is now needed - nor is it acceptable to growing numbers of people.

Two recent, authoritative and thoughtful accounts of modern society have suggested that social exclusion is increasingly based around exclusion from communication and information networks and that the roots of economic exclusion lie in social exclusion. Castells (1996) and Lash and Urry (1994) argue that we are now moving away from economies and societies based around physical stocks of assets to ones based around symbols and flows of information through networks, mainly based on fibre optics and computers, but also those that allow people to move freely and quickly to where the information is concentrated. Information technology has paradoxically resulted in the spatial concentration of those at the centre of information networks just as it has dispersed the routine functions associated with data inputting and management. These control functions now take place at the centres of city regions, of which London is one of the most important. Castells argues that some of the most cut-off places in this new world are likely to be the backends of what are currently the most 'advanced' cities. If nothing is done, East London is a prime candidate for such status not only to its own detriment, but also to that of the rest of London which will come to fear the threat it poses to their continued prosperity. East London has one of the lowest car ownership rates in the country and one of the worst planned public transport networks - its population is the least mobile in whole of London - making it unattractive to those who wish to live in an area which is easy to get in and out of but also to travel across. An e-mail address for every school child in East London and a web page for every school would be a start, as would the transport developments in the pipeline, which are outlined by Martin Simmonds and Abigail Warren in their article in this issue of the journal.

In some ways, East London starts off with a terrific advantage: traditionally it has been the upper and lower classes who have relied on networking. The former through the old boy network of public schools, the

City and West End clubs, and the latter through the informal organisations imposed by casual labour markets and part-time employment which characterised East London for much of the nineteenth and the first half of the twentieth century and which still survive today. Formal employment was a creation of Fordism which, for a short period after World War Two, gave security of tenure to the working and middle classes who have in turn discovered that this did not mean much when capitalism was faced with the problem of restoring profitability - as the working class discovered in the 1980s and the middle classes have (belatedly) realised also applied to them in the 1990s. If the latter have not lost their jobs, they have found their workloads doubling and learnt the definition of terms like flexibility, portfolio employment and multi-tasking the hard way. University lecturers have had to adapt to team-working, short-term contracts and to networking themselves into work groups within and across institutions. E-mail and the world wide web has transformed their lives enabling new ways of working. The longer term task of regeneration is to open up these networks and flows of information to those who are excluded from them and it is here that the education system has much to offer in East London.[1]

According to this argument, therefore, economic exclusion flows from social exclusion. This was in essence the message preached in the last issue of this journal by Greg Clark - that we have to do imaginative things to bring people into the area, to keep them here and allow them to talk to each other and most importantly to get those already here to talk to them. Stephen Timms argues in this issue that New Labour is thinking along some at least of the same lines. This has to be good. The key issue is that of social exclusion and it is here that the issue of regeneration has to date missed the point; although New Labour's New Deal gives some grounds for hope. Too much regeneration cash has gone to building things and too little to employing people. One example would be the very explicit way in which National Lottery money is allocated to capital projects and none is given to employing people directly, which means that some of the most worthwhile projects never reach the starting point given the way in which revenue budgets continue to be squeezed. The new campus in Docklands being built by the University of East London (and partners) from Single Regeneration Budget cash is an example. Only now is the university grappling with the real problems of providing jobs for local people and long-term education and training that will help ensure that East London does not become one of the new urban 'black holes' predicted by Castells. The danger is that a generation of senior managers who spent a decade downsizing and cost-cutting will be psychologically unable to grapple with the risks of creating something new which involves imagination and investment in people - for instance, along the lines proposed by Phil Cohen in his article in this issue.

Having said all of this, the minimum wage and other measures, outlined by Stephen Timms, should help to create jobs - at this stage what matters is jobs, any jobs almost - in an area where the economic inactivity rates approach 50 per cent in the wards surrounding UEL's new campus. Even if these jobs only last a few years building the campus or sweeping the station platforms or carrying the luggage of 'fat cats' arriving at London City Airport or the Stratford International Passenger Station, they should be welcomed. In particular, schemes that allow single parents access to high quality childcare whilst working and not to be worse off as a result are an absolute priority in an area where in some wards something like half the children are being brought up in households with only one parent. This is an area where the university might use some of its plant to good effect, not just in meeting a current need, but in 'normalising' the role of a university for people who might think it has no place to play in their lives, now or in the future. These are the immediate regeneration objectives.

The real problem however is to come: Newham, Hackney and Tower Hamlets have the highest birth rates in the country and the highest number of young people; they also have amongst the highest number of young people being brought up in families with only one parent. We know from the statistics already available that these people have the highest chances of doing badly at school (if they go at all) and of not being employed subsequently. This is the other problem to which I referred earlier: it is not just the 'middle class' trying to solve the problems of the 'under class', it is the middle-aged prescribing for a generation they know almost nothing about. At the University of East London it sometimes seemed that the planning for a modular degree structure was largely driven by the (different) perceptions of various senior staff of what their children wanted out of a degree scheme (not, it must be said, at universities like UEL). The old joke about treating research like a drunk uses a lamp-post - more for support than illumination - is particularly cutting when applied to a university committed to social research but at least UEL, unlike the majority of universities, does have a longstanding commitment to widening access. The problem is the research evidence would appear to point in different directions: Drew Stevenson, for instance, in our first issue cited work undertaken for Demos which suggested that young people's values were becoming more liberal, more tolerant of difference and more internationalist and that these 'leading edge' values were more prevalent in Britain than elsewhere. This caused my colleague Paul Watt to draw my attention to a recent survey undertaken by MTV (Music TV) on European youth which showed that British young people are the *least* tolerant in terms of attitudes to ethnic minorities in the whole of Europe - although they seemed to like having lots of sexual partners and taking drugs more! (Runnymede 1997). This failure to agree illustrates the huge problems involved in planning for a new generation. The point is that we don't know what the future holds, we don't know what our young people are like, all we do know is that telling them what the future will hold and what they must do to achieve that future will not work - again the tragic death of Princess Diana and its extraordinary aftermath point to this failure in communication between rulers and ruled. Essentially whatever interim measures we adopt (such as New Labour's New Deal on Welfare to Work) need to be predicated on one thing which is 'education, education and education' - primary, secondary and tertiary. It is also important that it is education with a small 'e'. All that Education with a large 'E' has achieved has been to ensure that the class system is reproduced, the occupational structure is properly serviced and that a small number of working-class kids are sponsored through into the professional middle classes and that if too many working-class kids appear to be doing well then new barriers are imposed, as for instance seems to be happening with the imposition of tuition fees in higher education. Education is not just about training, employment, inculcating 'values' or even skills acquisition (which in Britain of recent years has too often meant teaching an unwilling would-be workforce to wish those more fortunate than themselves to 'have a nice day' with varying degrees of convincing sincerity). Education is about fulfilling potential, it is about thinking conceptually and it is about learning how to use accumulated knowledge: no wonder IBM prefer to recruit history graduates rather than people with computer science degrees, especially from some of the ex-polytechnics.

As far as Education with a big 'E' is concerned, East London's core boroughs score top at being bottom - this was demonstrated by Vikki Rix in *Trends East* in issue 2 and the key facts are restated by Stephen Timms in his article in this issue. The implications of this are spelt out in Phil Cohen's article also in this issue which addresses the problem of building the new university campus in the Royal Docks - put crudely, more of the same won't work. We need a strategy which will ensure that most of those entering primary schools in East London this year will still be in education in fifteen years' time: it will involve a new approach to what education is for. The past is a guide to what went wrong, rather than to what went right.

'Equality of opportunity' and 'parity of esteem' were two of the buzzwords of the World War Two reforms that paved the way for the post-war welfare state. The political context was the pre-war dictatorships against which the war was being fought. It was recognised that their progenitor had been the failure of liberal capitalism to address issues of social justice and hunger. Equality of opportunity was not only a way of reconciling the market to social justice through the concept of meritocracy, but it was also a way of 'buying off' working-class dissent because everybody accepted that the educational reforms would take at least half a generation to work through and the benefits would only be realised by their children. This was largely what happened until a series of key studies showed what many already realised, which was that educational inequality was mapping on to social inequality and that the middle class were buying privilege through working-class taxation and that any mobility was simply a consequence of the growth in the economy and in non-manual employment. In other words, education was merely a filter to fit the number of people to the number of opportunities - at that time crudely, but effectively, measured by the number of university places which in turn governed entry to the professional middle classes. However, and this is the crucial point, it provided a breathing space until the benefits of the economic expansion began to filter through. It also provided the skilled personnel for that expansion which could not be satisfied from the existing middle class reproducing itself. It was, however, in the sociology of education that the geography of inequality first became apparent - 'good schools' were found in 'good places'. Ironically (and arguably) the move to a comprehensive education system only compounded the problem with areas like East London losing their beacons of educational attainment and achievement as the former grammar schools became comprehensivised in a downward spiral of achievement. In more favoured areas, the grammar schools were either retained and/or the comprehensive schools became good schools or bad schools largely dependent on their particular catchment area. Suddenly it was realised that 'schools do make a difference', but the most powerful effect in relation to which schools did well and which did badly was the class composition of their intake. Good schools attracted good teachers and it was only in the 1980s that the causality got reversed to 'bad teachers make bad schools'. It would be a brave person who tried to formulate a policy to reverse this geography of disadvantage, but it would be a social fool and political coward who did nothing.

The attraction of a grammar school education was not what it taught, so much as what it offered: access to a university and hence to a middle-class profession. That was in the days when 5 per cent of children went to university; nowadays the participation ratio is nearer 30 per cent and rising (Dearing notwithstanding). We do not know what have been the class consequences of this massive expansion of the higher education over the last decade. The middle classes may now make up a near majority of the population but its conditions of life offer nothing like the lifetime security of forty years ago: 'middle-class' jobs are increasingly of fixed term duration, are flexible, subject to 'speed up' and rationalisation. The advantages of having a university level qualification are in someways less (no passport to an automatic job), but the risks in not having a degree are considerably greater (no access to a decent job) whilst the scope of middle-class employment has changed out of all recognition. The other phenomenon is the massive feminisation of middle-class work. The Office for National Statistics is engaged in a major (and urgent) exercise in rewriting its occupational classifications to deal with this expansion of middle-class occupations and decline in working-class ones. Will Hutton (1995), has argued that Britain is now what he terms a 40:30:30 society with only the top 40 per cent having any security of tenure in employment and any prospects for the future - if this is the case then it seems reasonable to argue that this will increasingly map onto those with some form of further, higher or tertiary educational experience and qualifications. In this context, it therefore should be possible to offer the opportunity of educational success in ways that simply were not possible when only five per cent went to university. Of that five per cent only one in thirteen came from a working-class background who then found themselves whisked off into what were in effect finishing schools - a colleague of mine tells the story of having to lose her Geordie accent more or less overnight to survive at one of the radical new campus universities in the early 1960s.

When Paul Willis (1977) wrote his pathbreaking study of why working-class boys fail in the education system *Learning to Labour*, he was able to show that it was in fact the system that was failing the kids and not the other way around and that kids used the education system and its in-built class bias to learn the techniques necessary to survive in a capitalist labour market. He also showed how most of them regretted their educational strategy after a few years at work, despite the fact that they realized that they were in fact being set up for failure. Mentoring schemes already exist at UEL for black and asian students but somehow nobody thinks this might be appropriate for white working-class boys - arguably the most 'at risk' group in South Newham. Without such schemes, a Willis-type study of East London might be entitled *Learning to Deal* - how to work the drugs and other informal economies of East London. Dick Hobbs (1988) has more or less written such a book, but one written in another ten years will be considerably more vicious and less charming than the picture he paints of the East London villain. Education has to become everyday which means for example that pupils should be able to access the UEL campuses day or night to use the Internet, the cafe, the music labs or the learning resource centres.[2] The longer term aspects of the regeneration process need to find ways of facilitating lifelong learning not as some way of making everybody feel ignorant and that they need to go back to university to top up on skills, but as a way of encouraging youngsters to treat university as somewhere where they will normally expect to go. One could think of all sorts of ways of encouraging this - half-term schemes, summer schemes, inviting primary school kids to use the labs etc. As the quotation from Susan Brownill towards the beginning of this editorial suggests, Carole Snee and David Albury have perhaps put together the most thought-out strategy yet for the role the university can play in making education work in East London. To quote:

> I would recommend anyone in higher education to read David Albury and Carole Snee's final chapter which discusses the role of and challenges to universities in cultural and economic redevelopment. The ideas put forward here about universities truly serving local populations, about the reformulations of the aims of higher education to integrate it into a regeneration strategy and the struggles and compromises in achieving this provide much food for thought and also inspiration.

We must be doing something right! We run the danger of trying to use the regeneration issue to create a middle-class benevolent society where more resources go to those designing and evaluating the schemes than to those who should benefit from them, but given the above arguments that is not such a disaster as it might have been. *Rising East* can point to three volumes worth of ideas about ways in which the sub region can take advantage of the opportunities now being created by New Labour's New Deal and hopefully can avoid some of the threats it poses too. It is perhaps here that we have most to learn from our history and our failure to address that is something that we need to rectify in future issues. In the meantime, what we see as a regeneration strategy *is* a set of alliances and partnerships and it is to be hoped that *Rising East* has already played a role in bringing some of these together.

Turning to the contents of this issue, many of which have already been referred to, we have in the first section four articles. The lead article 'The Road to Beckton Pier?' is by Phil Cohen, who is director of the Centre for New Ethnicities Research (CNER) at the University of East London. In this long piece he provides a not uncontroversial analysis of the 'place' in the cultural geography of East London of the new campus which the university is building in what used to be the Royal Docks. He argues that we need to think very seriously about what it means to offer higher education opportunities in an area which has traditionally been at best apathetic and at worst antipathetic to higher education. In particular, he considers the implications of this development for the ethnic politics of the area: if we leave things as they are, white, black and Asian people could find themselves alienated from the education on offer. His prescription is that we need to rethink what it means to be a student which to date has been something which such people have not been brought up to think of as 'ordinary'. It is a thought provoking piece which, one hopes, will be seen as a major contribution to the building of this important new facility. In future issues we hope to carry more pieces of research that the university has funded as spin off from its development strategy.

John Eade and Chris Mele's article 'Global Processes and Customised Landscapes: the "Eastern promise" of New York and London' is a comparative study of the East End in London and East Village in New York. It demonstrates how the 'back ends' of two global cities have - so far - developed in rather different ways. East Village has succeeded in becoming a centre for cultural industrial workers and a centre for specialised production sustained by and sustaining an appropriate cultural infrastructure and a social mix involving gays, Puerto Ricans and others. This has not happened in London - yet. The Isle of Dogs has been very much a 'top down' development, often orientating itself to flight capital from the Asia Pacific region looking for a pied à terre in London or else to those working in the mainstream financial services industry. There has been little contact between these people and the indigenous population, both white and Asian. There is rather more hope for the other area studied - Spitalfields - where the authors identify the beginnings of cultural productivity. Clearly there is much to learn from East Village.

Martin Simmonds and Abigail Warren both work at the London Planning Advisory Committee (LPAC) and in their article, 'Re-addressing the East-West Balance: LPAC's East London Development Focus', they bring us up to speed on the considerable flow of initiatives currently taking place or mooted for our sub region and how these fit into an overall London strategy. This is likely to prove an extremely valuable context for the other more prescriptive articles we have carried on strategy: much is already underway or ready to start given the political will and/or the cash.

In 'East London and the New Labour Government', Stephen Timms, who is the Member of Parliament for East Ham, pulls together the various strands of Labour policy in the context of East London. What he points to is a window of opportunity to do something both short- and long-term for our sub region. Whilst Tony Blair has spent a lot of time downplaying expectations about what can be achieved, the Government has committed itself to getting East London back to work, into school and out of despair. However, the achievement of this will depend on the people of East London doing things for themselves rather than waiting to have them done for them.

Trends East is edited in this issue by David Dundon-Smith from LETEC. It is about business trends in the sub region and is based on the latest business surveys for the whole of the capital which have been commissioned by the London TECs. What it shows is the familiar picture of East London lagging behind the rest of London but it also shows that the demand is there for skilled employment and the need for organizations concerned with training and education to respond to that need with imagination and flair. Building on the previous two *Trends East* sections which were concerned with labour market trends and education, we feel that we have concluded our first year with a comprehensive survey of the human capital needs and resources of the East London sub region.

Hoxton Square features on our front cover and in his article in *Artyfacts*, Andrew Attfield assesses the re-invention of Hoxton as a cultural quarter by Hackney's City Challenge project. A fantastic success with exciting and high profile cultural industries basing themselves there, but what about the local inhabitants and their relationship to it all? These are timely questions in light of the popularity of cultural quarters in inner city regeneration projects all over Britain. In the nineteenth century Bethnal Green was the site chosen by the Victorians to open the prestigious East London Museum of Science and Art and the procession of royalty to attend its opening in 1872 was unprecedented in the East End. In '*Welcome to the East*', Cathy Ross explores the meanings of the setting up of the museum - can we see it as an agent of social change or was its exhibition of backward-looking objects a signal that the prevailing view was that the area had no future? Liz Greenhalgh looks forward to the Millennium celebration at Greeenwich, *A Date With Destiny* as she dubs it. Her article reveals the political shenanigans behind the scenes which she argues point to a new direction for cultural policy in Britain, led by entrepreneurs and not the Arts Council.

In her review of *Lara* by London writer Bernardine Evaristo, Nana Yaa Mensah unravels the story of a young girl from Woolwich and her attempt to construct a new identity for herself in a multiracial metropolis. Finally, we are proud to pay tribute to the passing of an East Ender who contributed so much to the cultural life of London, Stanley Reed a former director of the British Film Institute.

Tim Butler

REFERENCES

Brownill, S., (1997) 'Review of *Rising in the East*' in *Urban Studies*, Vol. 34 Number 8: 1320-1322.

Butler, T. and Rustin, M., (eds), (1996) *Rising in the East? The regeneration of East London*, London, Lawrence and Wishart.

Castells, M., (1996) *The Rise of Network Society*, Oxford: Blackwell.

Hobbs, D., (1988) *Doing the Business: Entrepreneurship, the Working Class and Detectives in the East End of London*, Oxford: Oxford University Press.

Jenkins, C., and Sherman, B., (1979) *The Collapse of Work*, London: Methuen.

Lash, S., and Urry, J., (1994) *Economies of Signs and Spaces*, London: Sage.

Willis, P., (1977) *Learning to Labour*, London: Gower.

The Runnymede Bulletin, (Feb 1997), No. 300.

NOTES

1. It is, of course, perfectly possible to argue that this is what has always happened - ask the working class to become more like the middle class and then shift the goal posts - but on the assumption that the changes that have been taking place over the last decade represent a qualitative shift, then there can be no doubt that we are moving from the industrial to the information age and skills and attitudes will have to move too.

2. If paying to keep the campus open for such purposes is the twenty-first century equivalent of digging holes in the 1930s, then so be it.

Urban regeneration and the polyversity[1]

The road to Beckton Pier?

Phil Cohen

> Mr Orwell was set down in Wigan for quite some time and it did not inspire him with any wish to vilify humanity. He liked Wigan very much - the people, not the scenery. Indeed he has only one fault to find with it, and that is in respect of the celebrated Wigan Pier, which he had set his heart on seeing. Alas! Wigan Pier has been demolished, and even the spot where it used to stand is no longer certain.
>
> *George Orwell*

When George Orwell went to Wigan to write his book on the condition of the English working class in the midst of the 1930s depression, he was following a well worn trail. As he trudged round the back streets, sampled the pubs and doss houses, fished for information amongst the unemployed staked out along the canal, he was walking in the footsteps of generations of middle-class reformers, religious and political missionaries, novelists and public commentators, who also went in search of some principle of redemption to be found in the depths of immiseration.

Orwell, for all his scepticism about socialism, and his deep-rooted class ambivalence, travelled hopefully. He expected to arrive at some approximation of the truth about his experience en route, even to happen upon glimpses of a better world emerging from the shadows of urban dereliction. But there is a downside to this picture. Orwell's very sensitivity to the sights and smells of poverty, his nose for detail about how life was lived on the other side of the tracks, sometimes led him astray. For as many critics have pointed out, he had a bad habit of only finding what he was looking for, and he only looked for what he though would confirm his own best hopes or worst fears about the working classes.

Today we cannot afford to be so innocent, or so hopeful about our motives, or the outcome of our research. We are more alert to the voyeuristic implications of urban exploration, have a sharper nose for the intricate impasses and subterfuges linked to persistent inequalities of gender, race and class. Nevertheless mounting pessimism of the intellect has proved no counterweight for resurgent optimisms of the will, especially when these have little purchase on political reality. Indeed, as Freud, rather than Gramsci, first made us see, wishful thinking - that special form of unconditional optimism - requires and thrives on the frustration of hope; it is not so much an antidote to disappointment as its secret ally.

This should at least caution us to avoid extremes of sentiment, as we look forward into the dawn of a new 'one nation' Labour administration. When it comes to considering what this historical compromise between two great conservatisms - the possessive individualism of Middle England and the more collective but no less possessive loyalties of working-class communities - might deliver in terms of actual governance, neither elation, nor despair seem called for. If, as Will Hutton (Hutton 1997) has persuasively argued, there is much in the programme of constitutional reform and in the concept of stakeholding that is promising, there is also clearly much work to be done to create the appropriate conditions for any of these promises to be delivered.

A similar caveat must apply to the prospect of a new university campus in East London. More than is usually the case, the campus that is about to be built on the site of the old Royal Docks, is a prime site for the projection of all kinds of hopes and fears, expectations, and anxieties, many of them belonging to conflicting interests and priorities. There is always the temptation to promise more than can be delivered, to try and make the new place mean all things to all people. There is the risk of believing one's own propaganda, and not facing up to some of the more difficult issues. There are the hard facts of the squeeze on public finance and the ever increasing competition for student numbers. There is the existence of a two tier system of higher education, with the high fliers, staff as well as students, still being drawn to the older universities even though they may in many cases be better served by the new. And there is the deep legacy of poverty, unemployment, racism and crime in an area that has suffered more than most under eighteen years of Tory rule. For all these reasons there is an almost irresistible urge to hope that a brand new hi-tech campus in docklands will tackle all these problems at a stroke.

But if anything has been learnt over these last years of short term opportunism, it is that investment in any enterprise only pays off as part of a much longer term strategy. As Drew Stevenson has insisted in this journal, the new campus cannot offer a quick fix for local problems in Newham, pressing as these are; its pattern of development must dovetail with a strategy of regeneration for the region as a whole. If there is a role for academics in this, it must involve facilitating public debate about these longer term aims and wider objectives.

At the same time a certain kind of long-termism can be as paralysing in its way as its opposite. People may become so aware of the precedents for failure, so conscious of the pitfalls at every turn, that they become daunted by the task and never begin. The new safety first code says: don't take any initiative that cannot be underwritten by cast iron guarantees. This attitude is hardly surprising, given that we are living in a world where the calculation of risk and insurance against it has become a highly profitable industry in its own right. Most people do not want to travel hopefully, they want to arrive. On time, and without any hassles on the way. They plan their career trajectories with almost astronomic precision, and if something goes wrong, they consult an astrologer to see if magic will fix it where the appliance of 'reason' has failed. In an increasingly chaotic world, uncertainty and the unknown are seen as bad risks. The questions asked about 'the state we're in' or 'what's up' are only ever the safe ones whose answers can be estimated in advance. The danger of the 'risk society' spawned by free enterprise capitalism is that people lose the very sense of adventure that is supposed to be its supreme virtue. (Beck 1992, Beck *et al* 1994).

In what follows I have tried to avoid these dangers while taking the risk of exploring the potential space for debate about the role of the university in urban planning that has been opened up by the building of this new campus. En route, I have become aware of how much has changed about the scale of our hopes since Orwell was writing. The conceit of Wigan-on-Sea, the only mill town in Britain to be billed as a pier head attraction, is a supreme example of optimistic northern working-class humour; it is an in-joke confident enough in local aspirations for a better life amidst the muck and grime, to poke fun at itself. Subsequently, the student generation of 1968 would have to dig much deeper into their imaginative resources to find the beach under the paving stones (Melucci 1989).

Today, in Docklands, the trope of 'the pier that never was' has come to stand not only for the destruction of a form of dock labour tied to a bygone age of industry and empire but also for the collapse of ambitions that lead beyond it, to a more equitable distribution of work and pleasure. Now, suddenly, after a long period of dereliction, several new piers and jetties are planned for the Royal Docks, as if the new campus wants to stake its own claim to a body of water that once provided a berth for international commerce and trade. Does this signal the beginning of a new kind of working waterfront, plugged into the global information flow or will it merely provide an ornamental backdrop for use in promotional literature? What story will the students who throng the new campus quays be able to tell themselves about the place and its purposes?

A tale of two campuses

SCENE ONE: RISING IN THE EAST

The new Docklands campus is an academic phoenix rising from the ashes of the old industrial East End to give birth to a bold new vision of the area's future. Situated on a prime waterfront location, and comprising an exciting mix of technology, design, the arts and cultural industry, the new campus offers students from a wide mix of backgrounds a superb range of facilities, including purpose built accommodation, a cinema and visual arts centre, watersports, and easy access to central London via DLR and the Jubilee Line extension. The presence of this vibrant multicultural community is of direct benefit to local people in Newham, creating jobs, widening access routes into higher education and providing recreational facilities which are so badly needed. Finally the campus is contributing in a major way to the economic regeneration of East London, promoting new partnerships with business and giving a focus to the Thames Gateway. This is a campus with a handle on the new millennium, offering a new image and fresh hope to an area which has in the past been blighted as much by official neglect as by its own bad reputation.

SCENE TWO : THE DECLINE OF THE WEST

The senior management of the University of East London held an emergency meeting last night to discuss what steps to take following a further incident on their new Docklands campus.

The campus has been built in a post industrial wasteland, created by the closure of the docks, the failure of the LDDC to develop an adequate strategy to replace lost jobs, and an opportunistic regeneration policy based on flagship cultural projects aimed at marketing the area's image to global investors, who have, however, largely failed to materialise.

The site itself is sandwiched between the noise corridors of City Airport and a major trunk road; staff and students have found themselves socially as well as geographically isolated and living on the front line of deep rooted antagonisms amongst the local community towards the new campus and what it represents. The failure of a previous plan which promised large scale employment opportunities has left many local people bitter or indifferent to what they see as an unnecessary facility designed largely for the benefit of an already privileged middle class. Much of this hostility has been directed against black, Asian and overseas students who make up a high proportion of the resident and travelling student body.

> As a result of these problems, additional security measures have had to be installed to protect the new campus from vandalism and theft, and students from mugging and racial attack. Particular efforts have been made to exclude drug dealers who have been drawn to the new campus where recreational drug use provides one of the few means of escape from the bleak surroundings. Unfortunately these measures have only succeeded in worsening tension. This is a campus under siege in every sense of the term. Not for the first time the planner's dream has turned into an nightmare for those who are forced to live and work in it.

These are both fictions, albeit of a different order. The first is what we would all like to believe will happen. The second is what some of us fear just might. How should these two stories be read against one another? We could relate them as a cautionary tale about the failure of a certain model of urban regeneration to take sufficient account of sociological realities. We could see it as yet another instance of the gap in imagination between planning and implementation; or, more philosophically, as the effect of an inevitable discrepancy between map and territory. We could regard these as best case and worst case scenarios, and hope that reality will turn out to be somewhere 'in the middle'.

There is however a more alarming possibility; the kind of wishful thinking that could produce the authorised PR version in the first case, might actively contribute to the outcome described in the second. The civic triumphalism naturally enough associated with the rising of a new campus in the East End of London might be its own worst enemy. It might contribute not so much to a renewal of the western university through its 'multiculturalisation' as to a decisive defeat for the whole project of giving working-class and minority ethnic communities a greater stake in higher education.

This would clearly be a disastrous outcome with more than local repercussions. It has frequently been pointed out that the very reason why financial support has been forthcoming for the new campus - namely the present dereliction of the Royals site, and the high levels of economic and social disadvantage in this area of East London, is also a major reason why the project could fail, unless the very process of building this new place entailed a fundamental change in the terms and conditions of its cultural and political geography.

This is a challenge which requires us to rethink not only the traditional western model of the university, but the process of urban regeneration itself (Cohen 1996a,1996c). I will look at the dominant model of urban regeneration in which universities are accorded an important role; more specifically I will question the claims currently made for cultural industries as a means to reconcile global forms of capital accumulation and investment with the no less urgent need to reconfigure and reskill local communities of labour. In the light of this analysis I will look at some emergent forms of labour and learning in the era of 'multicultural capitalism' and consider ways in which the polyversity might in principle stake out new contexts of aspiration and achievement for East Londoners.

The place of the university

Place-building is always conflictual and the struggle is always a struggle over the meaning of local histories and their relation to possible futures; it is about access to the symbolic resources of identity, which in turn entail claims of entitlement to material amenity and resource. The issue is never just about bricks and mortar, it is about the terms and conditions of stakeholding. Secondly, although the 'local' usually appears as something fixed and inert, and opposed to the dynamism of the global, the instances of dis- and re-location constitute a powerful, if unstable, dialectics of change; place-building always constructs new local subjects, new narratives of location, new and often contradictory meanings within a changed space of representation. Even the most green greenfield site is never a tabula rasa - it operates within a cultural geography which it modifies by its very presence. What kind of a place is a university campus? What makes building this place distinctively different from the construction of a museum or a factory, or a school, to take the three most common analogies to its function?

The most obvious answer is that its local subjects are defined by their possession of certain formal academic qualifications, and legitimated by their acquisition of even more qualifications. People who lack these entry tickets may live and work on or in the immediate vicinity of the campus, they may be directly or indirectly its beneficiaries, the administration and physical maintenance of the plant may depend on their labour, but using this criterion they are not local subjects and do not contribute to the public meaning of the place.

Secondly, the criteria which inform the regulation of university culture and the knowledges it transmits, are held to be universalistic - they do not in principle take account of any particularisms of birthplace or identity. Higher education is today all about meritocracy and sponsored mobility; it is supposed to enable students to go places, to become transnational subjects who transcend the specific gravity of local histories and geographies, and find themselves at home everywhere in the new space of information flows. Yet how far is this equation between universal (history) and global (geography) a compact with an already privileged minority?

Until very recently most universities recruited a highly selective intake of staff and students, overwhelmingly white, male and upper middle class. The habitual assumptions and social routines of academic life served to reproduce the hidden curriculum and invisible pedagogies associated with the closed transmission of cultural capital as a patrimony of knowledge and taste exclusive to the governing elite. A minority of people from outside these circles were admitted on condition that they assimilated to this essentially aristocratic culture of learning (Bourdieu 1984, 1994).

Before we consider how far all this has changed with the advent of the new 'polyversities', there are a number of things we need to recognise about the traditional model. Firstly local loyalties to the *alma mater* aim to have a global reach. The alumni associations of our 'ancient' universities constitute powerful networks of patronage and preferment whose pull extends through the British state and civil society and reaches around the English-speaking world.

Then there is the fact that the settlement of academic staff and students in and around the campus creates an extended middle-class residential community that appropriates certain elements of localism to preserve its claims to privileged amenity and resource. The local real estate market is, of course, one of the prime beneficiaries of this process of academic 'gentrification'.

Finally, and mostly importantly the concentration and interaction of local subjects on campus functions as a central element in narratives of global place-building. The foundation myths of the academic institution and its culture of collegiality support the fiction that this is a community of scholars engaged in the disinterested pursuit of truth, who at the same time, equip graduates to go out and become captains of industry, international civil servants, or leaders in the professions.

How then do universities locate and localise populations who are not strictly speaking its local/global (i.e. educationally qualified) subjects, but who may be required to service its operation? These populations are generally from working-class and/or minority ethnic backgrounds and the university has traditionally exploited their presence in two main ways.

Firstly they are targeted as sources of recruitment for non-academic staff - porters, cleaners, secretaries, maintenance workers, technicians, cooks, ancillary staff of every kind. Like any subordinate service class, their role is to keep things running smoothly behind the scenes. This does not however make them into local subjects; they do not perform cultural labour 'on site', and hence do not figure in the process of place-building. This official invisibility does not, of course, mean that they do not count. Non-academic staff find other ways of asserting identity, chiefly by carving out little niches of autonomy for themselves in the interstices of institutional life.

Secondly they are used as objects of research. Populations who live within easy travelling distance of the campus can expect to find almost every aspect of their personal, and social lives come under investigation. Their health and marriage patterns, their sex lives and reading habits all are grist to the academic mill. This does not normally make them local subjects; their role as informants is simply to provide the raw data which is transformed by students and staff into cultural capital, accruing to the professional reputation of the researchers and to the public name - and meaning - of the university. This process is often mystified by research rhetorics which talk about the long-term benefits to the wider community, or even to the informants themselves, but such payoffs are neither estimable, nor do they enter into the short-term calculations of those who volunteer their services. They do so, in the main, because their role as informants simulates a form of legitimate peripheral participation in the production of knowledge, a role they have been otherwise denied by the educational system.

There are a number of ways these populations may legitimately assert their claims as local subjects. They may challenge the cultural bias in selection procedures by seeking to enter the university as students. And they may engage with those university policies which directly affect local resource and amenity as representatives of community interests which have a stake in them. There is also a third way. The campus may be incorporated within the local hidden economy as a source of rich pickings thus mirroring the predatory or parasitic relationship which the university is felt to entertain with its servant classes.

Increasingly that relationship has been shaken up, and in a way that calls into question both the selective protocols of university culture and exclusionary strategies of urban regeneration. At the same time the customary forms of resistance that both white and black working-class young people have evolved in the context of their marginalisation by the education system are becoming increasingly redundant and dysfunctional. This phenomenon is especially pronounced in East London. I want now to look at some of the terms of transformation in the sub-region to see whether they foreclose or, more hopefully, open up new points of engagement with higher education that go beyond the model of local subjection I have so far outlined.

The old East End - a new cultural industry?

In the last ten years slash and burn strategies of urban regeneration have met with increased resistance from a widening consortium of interests (Bianchini 1988, 1993). In their stead a new model has been pioneered in which processes of 'spontaneous unslumming' hitherto associated with the gentrification of the old inner city, have been linked to the advent of a new information and entertainment-based economy operating on a global scale (Zukin 1988). Through the conversion of warehouses and small factories into offices, studios, flats, galleries, restaurants and shops, many of the traditional areas of manufacture have been transformed into hives of cultural industry where small businesses of every kind, especially those linked to the arts and the mass media, trade off each other's presence and help promote the 'global city'.

The 'old' East End has been a prime site for this transformation,

A ten-foot high wall between the social housing and adjacent 'urban village', July 1997. Photograph by Bruce Jerram.

comprising as it does an extensive waterfront and hinterland with a large number of premises suitable for conversion, and a resident population that provides both 'local colour' and a reserve army of low wage service workers (Butler and Rustin 1996). For we are talking here about the advent of a new, multicultural, form of capitalism, in which the accumulation process requires not only an internationalised flow of information and ideas from a diversity of sources around the world, but, the presence of diasporic networks of labour drawn from non-European cultures (Castells 1991). Let's briefly look at each side of this story in turn.

'Multicultural capitalism' - capitalism based on the production of cultural diversity and the marketing of the exotic - is at the cutting edge of globalisation (King 1995). It works by manufacturing particular goods and services associated with the cultural labour of local subjects, and packaging them for global consumption under the generic brand name of 'authentic ethnicity'.

This operation has thrown up a new fraction of the professional middle class that works in what has been called the cultural mass: a heady mix of pre-electronic arts, based on analogue forms, closely interfacing with digitalized informatic media. Unlike the inhabitants of 'Middle England' closeted in their xenophobia, this middle class both produces and consumes cultural diversity on a global scale, from world music to the latest in cross over fashions. And unlike the homogenised business culture promoted by multinational companies with their rigid dress codes and concern for 'corporate image', the lifestyles of this stratum advertise individuality, flair, difference - the same values they promote via their products (Sassen 1995).

The new wave of fashion designers, graphic artists, TV producers, media consultants, public relations people, copy writers *et al* tend to be educated at polyversities, not Oxbridge; they have grown up in and through the frenetic individualism of 1980s enterprise culture, not the team spirit instilled by the public school. This middle class is no longer dominated, either numerically or ideologically by white men. Women, and members of ethnic and sexual minorities have been in the vanguard. And like any emergent social force they have constructed a view of the world in their own image, a world in which there is no reality outside its representation, where diversity, or its current trendy analogue, hybridity, is celebrated and the pleasures of consumption are put at the cutting edge of change. En route, gender and race (but not class) have been transformed from topics of personal identity work into resources for consciously directed cultural production. Through the intervention of new rhetorics of entitlement, lifestyle innovation ceases to be merely an object of cultural labour, but a privileged means of

accumulating cultural capital. And this in turn earns a return on personal investment that can be measured in material terms.

This new fraction is a hybrid in another sense. It can be considered as a new aristocracy of labour in so far it exercises a high degree of creative control over the technologies it operates. At the same time, it merges the values of the premodern artisan with those of the post modern entrepreneur. Unlike the old 'self-made men' these do-it-yourself capitalists actively trade off their ethnicities or sexualities to give an added competitive edge to what is produced for the local/global market in 'travelling ideas'.

But this is only one half of the story. The structures that produce this new multicultural middle class also throw up, as its necessary counterpart, a new kind of working class. Cultural industries require and actively promote a dual labour market, where a highly paid professional service class coexists with and sometimes directly employs a low wage/low skill servant class made up of women, young people, recent immigrants and refugees and ethnic minorities. It is the pre-industrial labour of these 'hidden hands' that oils the post-industrial machineries of the cultural mass - from the bike couriers who deliver manuscripts or films to the seamstresses who sew the labels on designer jeans by hand, from the kitchen porters who staff the canteens of TV studios to the night cleaners who tidy the offices; as for the more visible economy it is students and unemployed cultural workers (actors, artists, writers) who are employed as front of house attractions in cafes, wines bars and restaurants

Britannia Water 'urban village' on the south side of Victoria Docks, summer 1997. Photograph by Bruce Jerram.

where their faces, and their arts of impression management, blend more acceptably into the middle-class *mise-en-scène* (Zukin *op cit.*; Sassen *op cit.*; King *op cit.*).

This multicultural labour force is more 'flexible' than the historically sedimented sections of the old manual working class, less entrenched in a fixed habitus of customary work practice, and hence easier to hire and fire. They are also major cultural innovators in their own right, continually introducing new topics of identity work, new hybridised styles of cultural labour which in turn provides the 'raw material' for cultural capitalism.

It is not the case that one 'class' lives literally at the expense of the other. The exploitative nature of the classical capital/labour relation is not directly reproduced but takes on a more mediated form. Cultural labour - the work of inscribing collective meaning and personal identity on whatever materials are selected for this purpose (music, clothes, bodies, motorbikes, walls etc.) - does not in itself create material value. It creates signs of authenticity and/or signatures of authorship. For these to function as marketable commodities they have first to be processed through a machinery of re-presentation. This is what cultural capital is and does: *it is the accumulated knowledge/power that intervenes to organise the commodification of cultural labour through its means of representation*. At the same time it transforms the topics of identity work into resources that can be traded or bargained over.

It is therefore possible in principle for the same individual or group to be on the side of cultural labour and capital at the same time, or to move continually between them. The imagined community of multicultural capitalism is, indeed, constituted by this constant to-ing and fro-ing, in which a kaleidoscope of signifying practices blurs the distinction between positions. Youth styles that trade off cultural diversity provide a key currency of 'free and equal exchange', or, if you prefer, mutual exploitation between the two 'sides' in a way that turns structures of inequality into a kind of secret pact. Thus young unemployed East Enders can trade drugs, music, and even insults with the young professionals who are making a fortune out of marketing their street cultures 'up west', without either side necessarily feeling that they are losing out.

The populist promise of cultural industries in the 1980s was precisely that cultural labourers could become cultural capitalists (Willis 1993). What was practised for pleasure could be practised for profit. Gay, black and even white working-class lifestyles could be turned into new means of livelihood. Gangstas would become rap stars, taggers would become graffiti artists, East End lads would follow in the footsteps of East 17, street market hipsters would become fashion designers and the denizens of the hidden economy would all be able to go straight and pay their taxes. The role of the polyversity in this context was to provide access routes into the special vocational skills and background knowledge that would make this transition possible.

Unfortunately the payoff has been less than hoped. For every media career that has taken off, there are dozens of has-beens and hundreds of wannabes, many of them with good degrees but working in banks or driving minicabs, still waiting for that big break. The notion that cultural industries could absorb a sizeable fraction of the labour power made redundant through corporate downsizing and technological shakeout proved to be wildly over optimistic even in the boom period of the 1980s.

In fact the cultural industries are a misnomer. Not only because the technical processes involved are post-Fordist, but because their growth has actually accelerated the process of de-industrialisation. As the old manufacturing districts went into terminal decline, the cultural industries moved in to repackage them for tourist and residential consumption. Surviving traces of labour history were incorporated as elements of 'local colour' within carefully postmodernised landscapes (Zukin 1991; Smyth 1994). For the urban imagineers who set out to sell docklands to prospective clients, the presence of the odd rusting crane and other remnants of dockside industry provided a 'quaint' quote from the past to counterpoint the environment of hi tech 'modernity' going up all around (Boyer 1994). The creation of special conservation areas, the marketing of Banglatown as post-imperial 'ethnoscape', the promotion of Bethnal Green as a folk museum of cockney custom, these are classic instances of cultural industry at work. Jack the Ripper, the Kray Twins, Gilbert and George, Bangladeshi Cockneys and the cast of Eastenders all have their walk on parts in this multi-media show which has invented a 'new' old East End as a site for gentrification by the new middle class.

Under favourable circumstances this process may help create that unique mix of the plebeian, the bohemian, and the ethnic on which student quarters seem to thrive: areas in which cafes, bookshops, clubs, and art galleries gain a foothold in converted, but still low cost, premises situated within run down multiracial neighbourhoods where housing and shopping are also cheap.

In general though, the dual labour market that underpins multicultural capitalism produces a new form of the dual city. Although principles of residential segregation still apply, they take on a much more complex and fragmentary form than in the past. The presence of low cost housing on often run-down council estates alongside expensive luxury apartments and private housing developments has produced a highly racialised geography in the old East End (Massey 1991). The much vaunted 'multiculturalism' of these areas not only glosses over the juxtaposition of yuppie wealth with largely black and Asian poverty; it conceals the widespread and complex nature of 'white flight' that has been going on in the interior of the old working-class city.

To understand what is stake here, we have to do more than acknowledge the historical decline of manual labourism and the closure of the docks. We have to look at how structural change is being negotiated in and through the way these cultures and communities continue to be reproduced.

With the decline of industrial Fordism, informal apprenticeships to patrimonies of skill centred on the manual trades no longer have any basis of support in the workplace culture. But they continue to be transmitted through families, where they not only shape narratives of aspiration, but actual adolescent transitions (Cohen 1997b). As a result the customary configuration of gender roles in the family sets a template for identity work which no longer corresponds to the sexual and generational division of labour in the most dynamic and growing sectors of the economy. The cultural labour of girls remains ever more confined within the domain of the matrilocal, whilst boys, in order to escape from its clutches, stake out territories of masculine rivalry and defiance on its borderlands. Here other topics (and topoi) of identity work, such as whiteness and Englishness, are available. But however much race may become a compensatory object of cultural labour, there is, fortunately no capital to be made out it. No one makes it big in any eyes other than their own or their 'mates' by beating up blacks. As for sexism, the labours of masculinity associated with 'laddism' may be fashionable for the middle-class readers of *Loaded*; but in the real world, East End lads have the greatest difficulty in taking up the new opportunity structures offered by formal education and the cultural industries; meanwhile the traditional transition routes into work lead into the promised land of job security and the family wage only for the favoured few; the rest enter the casual labour market, the hidden economy, and chronic long-term unemployment, dreaming of life in the fast lane.

The new form of urban dualism reinforces this pattern of disadvantage. Those who are at home, as local subjects, in the global city, and who have a long-term investment in its future are able to plan ahead and develop flexible networking strategies that enable them to gain effective purchase on urban decision-making structures. But those who are trapped in defensive emplacements and narratives are cut off from these more mobile resources of power. The decline in the political culture of labourism means that an increasing number of the white working class now have little experience or confidence in making plans for anything but their most immediate needs. To live wholly in the present is at least to be mobilised to deal with the exigencies of everyday living, which for many young East Enders has become an increasingly risky, and time consuming business. The alternative, taken by their elders, is to live in the past, since that at least can be controlled through selective memory. 'Old' labour, the white cockney communities of the East End, are by and large immobilised in a culture of nativist complaint; - yet the very terms in which they stake their claims to cultural insiderdom, makes them outsiders in the global city.

On the other side of the race tracks, the news is more encouraging. The younger generation of leaders now emerging from within black and Asian communities in East London is clearly at home in the global city, even if their parents are not. This is not just about an evident facility with the Internet and the mobile phone. Their access to new information technologies stems from a happy conjuncture between the extensive reach of diasporic narrative, and the intensive ambition of enterprise culture. These young men and women are going places in every sense of the word. For some at least the promise of the cultural industries, to create a framework that would transform the topicality of cultural labour into a material resource, has paid off. With a little help from the polyversity, and a lot of hard graft, they have made it into the multicultural middle class.

So we are dealing with a complicated pattern of race and class division, articulated through gender and generation. The process of urban regeneration has added its own specific structure of contradiction to the story. For at one level we have the reconstruction of an 'authentic multicultural core' associated with the 'old East End', and the simultaneous development of a large outer periphery where the 'old' white working class-in-flight has attempted to reconstitute their shattered culture. At the same time in the global city, the process of 'going with the flow' of multicultural capitalism undermines the whole spatial logic of the core/periphery model. The Thames Gateway, if it were ever to exist as a structure of meaningful place-building, would be entirely excentric to itself. There would be no room for the old hierarchies of place and identity. This would be a postmodern geography in which there were no longer any insiders or outsiders, only hybrids (Soja 1989).

It is indeed the case that the boundaries of East London are shifting under the feet of those who dance to more dis-orienting rhythms than Chas and Dave (Sharma *et al* 1997). The historic quasi-colonial relation between East and West is being reconfigured into a medley of sights, sounds and significations which cannot be placed or understood in terms of the old maps. Or the old local anthems to the nationalism of the neighbourhood. This creates special problems as well as possibilities for a university that is not just in but very much 'of' East London and it is to this we must now turn.

Ethnoscapes

What makes the University of East London (UEL) such an interesting place at the present time is that it is where the Old and New East End meet on ground of neither's making. Before we decide whether this encounter is likely to prove productive or not, it may be worth reminding ourselves of some of the key features of the terrain.

The eastward movement of white populations from the historical heartlands of the old East End around the docks began in the 1930s, and continued in the immediate post-war period, creating the so called the 'one class community' of Barking and Dagenham, built economically around Fords. Barking Tech with its four faculties of Science, Engineering, Domestic Science and Art, was as much a part of this community as the Dagenham Girl Pipers. In the 1960s and 1970s the cockney diaspora pushed into Essex and became increasingly a phenomenon of white flight from areas of Bangladeshi and, to

Down with the old, up with the new: West Silvertown becomes Britannia Water. Photographs by Bruce Jerram.

a lesser extent, Afro-Caribbean settlement in Tower Hamlets and Newham. At the same time the expansion of higher education, the transformation of Barking and West Ham Techs into the Polytechnic and then University of East London, pushed the institution increasing out of the reach of a local white working class who found themselves insulated within a shrinking, but nevertheless highly organised culture of manual labourism. At the same time a new opportunity structure emerged for the increasing numbers of Asian and black students living in East and North London, who did well enough at school to enter higher education. UEL increasingly became for them an academic home from home. But as local subjects of East London's very own academe, their presence was often resented by the white 'locals' of Barking and Dagenham who saw it as a case of the blacks taking over 'their old tech'.

The university thus occupies a highly racialised place in the cultural geography of East London. The potential for racial antagonism between its two main local student constituencies remains an ever present factor in the calculation of strategies for growth. There is a great deal of concern lest the 'Barking scenario' be repeated, with even more dire consequences, in Beckton.

The actual location of the new campus, sited as it is in an overwhelmingly white ethnoscape with a widespread, and not unjustified, reputation for racism, makes these anxieties entirely realistic. We have a potential scenario in which the new multicultural (black and Asian) middle class are attracted by what the campus has to offer but are put off by its siting in what they see as a racial no-go area, while the white communities who live on the doorstep may also experience the campus as beyond their academic reach: the worst of both worlds.

The problem is to some extent aggravated by the local site history. The Royal Docks were largely insulated from the rest of the area; the dockers themselves constituted something of a 'race apart' as well as forming, with the local gas workers, the backbone of a white labourism that fiercely resisted the presence of 'foreign' workers. On the closure of the docks, the infrastructure was demolished and the site taken over by the LDDC who initially envisaged it as a downriver, and perhaps down market, extension of Canary Wharf. That plan succumbed, like so much else, to the collapse of the property boom in the 1980s. The clearing of the site thus marked not so much the opening of viable new future for local people, as its foreclosure. A very white working-class history was erased and in its place was put precisely nothing. A landscape of dereliction and exclusion.

This long vacant site did not serve to trigger symbolic place-building activity amongst local people, because its potential meaning was simply not germane to their lives. Firstly none of these populations were structurally in a position to influence the planning process proactively. It was not for them to petition the council or the LDDC for a university campus to be built on their patch. They have not been consulted on any of the fundamental decisions which affect the campus development, nor will they be. They are simply not its local subjects. On the basis of some recent research using focus groups it seems that the main local priority is job creation. This again could be predicted but what people want is, at this level, immaterial. It is literally and figuratively speaking neither here nor there.

As things stand, then, the people of Newham may reap some secondary benefits by taking up opportunities for work in building and servicing the new site, or offering themselves up as objects of academic research, or stealing quantities of material, none of which disturbs the traditional relationships between the university and its servant classes. At the same time it is entirely possible that racialised resentment against the academic success of ethnic minorities may be directed against the local student body.

Faced with such a depressing prospect, anyone could be forgiven for deciding to forget about these communities and concentrate instead on firming up the offer to local subjects who belong to the global city and its international networks of investment. The synergy will be with hi tech enterprise and cultural flagship projects - a hotel, a conference centre, a visual arts centre - that will draw in the people, and the money from a wide area and so help create a truly cosmopolitan community of use in and around the site. These high fliers will put the campus on the map, and help attract a wider, more multicultural middle class and overseas student clientele whose fees will give the new venture a more secure financial base.

It all makes sense, and certainly some of these ingredients must feature strongly in any final plan. But the peculiarities of the site and its cultural geography militate against this solution. The elements of urban infrastructure, normally regarded as attractors for cultural industry, are neither present nor can they easily be created 'on site'. There is no 'local colour'. There is little or no potential for academic gentrification. Given the unprepossessing environment and the high levels of air and road traffic pollution there is unlikely to be extensive residential settlement by staff. They will commute in from more salubrious areas. Their children will not go to local schools and the local real estate market will not benefit. Finally there is neither the potential for the kind of cultural agglomeration that sustains a vital student quarter, nor the spaciousness and allure of a greenfield site.

For all these reasons the Docklands campus is unlikely to succeed as a multicultural enterprise unless its developmental role is rethought. Yet there is much in current thinking about both universities and urban regeneration that militates against any such critical re-appraisal.

Enter the polyversity

The shift in urban policy from social to cultural capital, from regeneration strategies centred on job creation and public housing to flagship cultural projects is mirrored by the rise of cultural and media studies in the place of the social sciences in universities during the 1980s. In principle this shift makes it easier to portray the new Docklands campus as a potential site of intersection between corporate culture and popular culture, art and industry, in a way that offers to bridge these ancient divides (Wynne 1993).

Even if it were not possible to gloss over the local effect of class and race inequalities for long, the promise of a more permeable relation between cultural labour and capital is enough to promote the polyversity as a key player in the urban regeneration game. In this scenario the campus becomes an important cultural and technical resource for local firms and communities, helping to retrain the local unemployed working class in new post-Fordist sectors and labour processes; the campus supports municipally backed regimes of 'empowerment' for marginalised and disenfranchised groups, by offering forms of vocational training geared into local situated knowledges, which are thereby disseminated, through skill transfer, upwards and outwards to the wider world.

This is an attractive model and one that is based on the historical precedent of popular planning set by the GLC. There are, however, important lessons to be learn from that experience. Although the aim was to democratise and widen access to planning processes, the main beneficiaries were in fact professional middle-class radicals (heavily disguised as community activists) who exercised a virtual monopoly over the knowledge networks required to operate effectively at this level. For the reasons I have outlined, a campus built around cultural industries would be unlikely to significantly redistribute cultural capital unless its whole structure of provision was changed.

The problem is that the work of undertaking any such a revision comes up against pressure from other quarters. In order to engage in place-building at all, to generate the kind of political and economic support required to get the campus off the drawing board and onto site, a quite different kind of urban regeneration game has to be played. The polyversity has to promote itself as a source of technological innovation, and technology transfer; in this scenario the campus functions as a local node in the global flow of capital in order to stimulate inward investment and population on a regional, national and international scale. Academe thereby stakes its claim as a leading institution of the global city. Its main clients and supporters are now multinational corporations, central government agencies, and transnational NGOs; regimes of knowledge dissemination are similarly based on disciplines with a global reach. There will, it is hoped, be some trickle down effect into the local economy, via the advent of a relatively affluent middle-class consumers into its midst.

In the mission statements that have so far been issued about the new campus, it is clear that elements from both upward transfer and trickle down models have been fused together in the effort to produce a public declaration of intent that will satisfy all parties. This will be a 24-hour campus built around hi-tech learning resources, serving the R&D needs of the most advanced sectors of the global economy whilst, at the same, it will offer the local working-class communities of Beckton and Canning Town the means to equip themselves with the skills they need to obtain secure, well paid, jobs within it.

The notion that there might be tensions, let alone contradictions, between these two aims is glossed over by appealing to the regenerative capacity of cultural industries. This in turn provides a rationale for 'partnerships in growth' that seem to reconcile public interest with private profit, and allow the polyversity to take a leading role in initiating cultural flagship projects : arts centres, heritage trails, industrial archaeology sites and the like. Finally the development of vocational training for cultural industries is aimed at a wide range of students, whilst the agglomeration of hi tech/arts/fashion, design, advertising and other media-based forms of higher education in an East London campus gives the global cultural economy an injection of local street cred.

It seems to be a winning formula, offering the best of all possible worlds. But is it really possible to have it both ways? Let us look a little more closely at what is at stake in the proposed merger between higher education and cultural industry.

Cultures of learning and labour

It is a characteristic of the 'new universities', compared with the old, that they bring together many different forms of knowledge/dissemination, some with a globalising and others with a localising scope and impress on them a common, if loose, coherence. It has been suggested that the polyversity is especially well adapted to the needs of multicultural capitalism. It is where particularised cultures of learning brought in by non-traditional students enter into dialogue with universalising cultures of teaching belonging to the traditionally educated white middle-class elite. This facilitates the emergence of new 'local global' forms of situated knowledge, hybrid regimes of truth that offer interdisciplinary homes from home for architects, engineers, mathematicians, historians, writers, artists and social scientists (and those who study with them) where they can become conversant with the convergent grammars of each others respective trades; whether in the study of fractal geometry, or tectonic plate geology, or the use of rhizomes, and butterfly attractors to model processes of social/cultural change, or the emergent arts of the Internet, there is a common enterprise which has, as its prime referent, topics of investigation which give priority to the *linkage* between local and global phenomena, rather than their separate or oppositional frames.

Now this is indeed a bold vision of the multicultural university and its educational future. Unfortunately it does not correspond to what actually goes on under present conditions, as staff grapple ever more desperately with a modularised curriculum that maximises consumer choice whilst minimising the resources required for true interdisciplinary endeavour, and where student cultures are often dominated by essentialist, ethnocentric agendas.

Of course the notion of higher education as a place and time where all kinds of intellectual and cultural cross currents meet and 'fertilise' one another is nothing new. It was a central tenet of the old liberal university. But in that case it was a matter of subsuming the newer, non-traditional knowledges under the old disciplinary hierarchies, as a means of renewing and extending their scope. Now we are faced with the much more risky and exciting task of putting into question the eurocentric epistemologies which have hitherto dominated the hidden curriculum of the western university whilst at the same time conserving what is useful in the enlightenment project (Cohen *et al* 1996a).

That rethinking of the global is what is required of a research culture capable of matching the challenge of the new campus. At the same time there is no ducking the task of finding new ways of enabling the communities living on the campus doorstep to see it as a site of relevant aspiration. Only then are they likely to become engaged in adding public meaning to the place, proactively and constructively, rather than reactively and destructively.

How then can we devise a model of the higher education curriculum that redefines the relation between its local and global subjects? One reason why the question seems so hard to answer is that we have literally been looking in the wrong place. We have been looking at what goes on in classrooms, in the process of academic dis/qualification, we have been looking at curriculum development and pedagogies, at what and how we teach. We have not been looking at how and what and where young people actually learn, in families, through friendships, in peer groups; we have not been looking at the local situated knowledge they acquire and transmit in these settings, the kinds of identity work this entails. Above all we have been looking at the problem from the vantage point of cultural capital rather than cultural labour.

How do young people learn to dance, or ride bicycles, play football, write graffiti, tell jokes, or tall stories, practise safe sex, use computers, play musical instruments? All of these activities could be described as involving a form of apprenticeship or initiation into a shared community of practice. This involves starting from the position of a newcomer or noviciate and gradually learning the rules of a particular language game, and/or a particular techniques of the body, through watching what other, more advanced, exponents of the skill do with it, listening to their counsel, and, of course, practising. Practising involves an element of mimetics - but this is not so much a matter of simple imitation or shadowing, but an active process of emulation fired by the desire to go one better. The teacher in this process is not so much a master, as a mentor, someone who can demonstrate by example, can indicate the step by step process which characterises the transformation of the noviciate into an 'old hand' and can tolerate the frustration *and* the ambition of the learner en route. The key point is that what is learnt and mastered is not just a skill but an identity, or rather a form of identity work. And this is an incremental process - in which the learner moves from a peripheral and passive role in the community of practice to an ever more central and active one (Lave 1991).

There are several aspects of this model which are useful in thinking about access routes into higher education. If non-traditional students are to identify with the new campus as site of realistic expectation, then it will be because they can literally envisage themselves as part of its student body and that depends on being offered a student identity that makes sense to them in terms of where they are 'coming from'. In order to take the first risky step, literally to read a brochure, or travel on the DLR to visit the site, they have first to be able to imagine themselves already there as one of its local subjects. The campus has to be part of the story they tell themselves about how their lives may go.

To put this another way, if the polyversity as a centre of multiple communities of practice does not offer an identity that makes sense as an extension of existing informal cultures of learning then its curriculum offer will not be taken up. It is a mistake to think that student identity is necessarily or primarily vocational - i.e. that people go to college to learn to become social workers, artists, engineers or whatever (Holland 1990). In the first instance what they learn, or fail to learn, is how to be students - and they learn how to be students from other students who have been at it longer and know the ropes. Academics think this is all about study skills. But actually it about *studenting* skills. This, for many people who do not come from a background in higher education is the hardest lesson of all to learn.

Unless there are mentors already in place to help newcomers acquire these skills, they are unlikely to master then and this in turn will affect their academic performance. Mentors in this context are peers who have mastered appropriate forms of cultural labour or identity work. And here we come up against a curious paradox. We know what a black or Asian student identity is about, partly because mentoring schemes have been put in place to help these students assert these specific cultural identities and there are strong ethnically-based student organisations. But we do not know what a working-class student identity looks like. Indeed it strikes us as a kind of oxymoron - students may 'come from working-class backgrounds', but their move into higher education seems to involve them in surrendering that as a foreground identity; if they are also white, then their presence or absence is not recognised as an equal opportunity issue, they are simply subsumed within the cross (or non) class category of race. In other words, the racial body count renders contradictory class locations invisible. The development of an informal peer group mentoring scheme for these students would thus seem to be an essential provision for the new campus.

The building of the campus must also be treated as an opportunity for generating situated knowledge that goes beyond the local, or rather places it within the widest possible sense of the world. That means every aspect and phase of the site construction has to be used as a learning resource for young people in local schools. At one level this would involve university staff working with primary and secondary school teachers to devise new curriculum projects using the place-building process to explore a range of environmental, social, geographical and historical issues pertinent to the new economy of signs that is under construction.

At another it might involve exploring what might realistically constitute a working waterfront. Here UEL is in a strong position to draw in elements of the black and Asian enterprise culture, by gearing educational provision directly into the process of capacity building. The death of the old docks-based community of white labourism might then be seen to be a precursor to the redevelopment of a properly multicultural waterfront in which the black Atlantic carried the full freight of its history into the making of new times.

The building of the new campus also offers an opportunity to extend the scope of public arts to articulate the collective memory of what has been lost or erased in this historic shift. That does not have to mean engaging in some cynical, or nostalgic act of retrieval: the display of a few relics to remind us that this was once a dockyard. The exploration of the 'past as a foreign country' has to be integrated into a sense of what realistic futures can be envisioned and imaginatively sketched out through an educational process in which young East Enders feel they have an active, material stake.

These are a few examples of the way in which the inevitable experience of dislocation can be put to work in creating a more open ended and positive process of relocation. And here the university itself can give a lead through its own internal practice. Campus relocation is not a simple administrative matter. It is not just about the allocation of office space, or the provision of staff and student facilities. There is more to moving to Docklands than ordering the removal vans and transporting this or that existing department of knowledge to a new site. It should involve a lengthy, and not always pleasant process of first dislocating and then reconstructing the present curriculum and culture of the polyversity in order to engage more effectively with the evasive inequalities of multicultural capitalism. This is the only way to begin to sketch out an alternative design on the future that makes the new campus a genuine part of the stakeholder project.

The Road to Beckton Pier

The university has to struggle with the twin task of meeting the rising expectations of the black and Asian communities in East London and elsewhere, whilst at the same time attempting to refocus the aspirations of white working-class pupils who seem to be largely indifferent to its educational charms but who are deeply resentful that others are taking advantage of them. The challenge then is to create opportunity structures that facilitate the emergence of new communities of aspiration cutting across hitherto firm boundaries of class, gender, nation and race. I have tried to show that the dangers of not setting out to travel hopefully on this path are greater than the risks of doing so.

Which brings us back to where we began, with George Orwell. Perhaps, after all, with hindsight, *The Road to Wigan Pier* does lead us from old to new labour. If you go to Wigan today you will find that it now does 'in reality' have a pier. At least it has a place called by that name in memory of the cantankerous old Etonian who put the town on the map. Wigan Pier today consists of a converted warehouse by the old canal which houses a museum of local labour history. The visitor enters a series of built environments that simulate a 'world we have lost'. You can crawl on your hands and knees to the coalface, without getting your hands dirty. You can be taught in an Edwardian school room without getting ink on your fingers. You emerge from this sanitised version of working-class life and go into a postmodernist cafe/shop across the way where you can buy toys made out of bits of old spinning looms and eat traditional Lancashire Hotpot. At the end of the visit you go away feeling grateful that times have changed for the better.

For better or worse we do not have the means to create this kind of material illusion in the Royal Docks. We have a more down to earth and potentially lethal reminder of the past on our doorstep. The proximity of the new site to the old Beckton gasworks has created its own specific legacy. Gas has apparently seeped though into the subsoil and there is the risk in drilling the new foundations that some of this toxic waste will be released. No doubt steps will be taken to ensure that this does not happen. But it furnishes us with a compelling metaphor for the risk we run of a return of the historically repressed that might yet poison the local atmosphere. An all too dangerous example of how the material and symbolic dimensions of place-building coalesce.

An earlier version of this text was presented to a meeting of the East London Forum at the University of East London. I am grateful for the opportunity to present some of these ideas to such an informed and critically engaged audience. Subsequent discussions with Tim Butler, Mike Rustin and Bruce Jerram have also contributed considerably to the clarification of the argument. None of the above should however be held at all responsible for the views expressed here. The theoretical model, on which this paper is based, is developed in the full version of this paper, available from CNER, University of East London, Longbridge Road, Dagenham, Essex RM8 2AS.

This text also serves as a background paper for a community arts and education project linked to the new Docklands campus. The project is being developed jointly by the Centre for New Ethnicities Research (CNER) and the Art and Design dept. at

UEL. Further information about this project can be obtained by writing direct to CNER at the University of East London.

REFERENCES

Appadurai, A., (1997) *Modernities At Large*, Chicago: Chicago University Press.

Beck, U., (1992) *The Risk Society*, London: Sage.

Beck, U., Giddens, A., Lash, S., (1994) *Reflexive Modernisation*, Cambridge: Polity.

Bianchini, F., (1988) *City Centres, City Cultures*, Manchester: Manchester University Press.

Bianchini, F., (1993) *Cultural Policy and Urban Regeneration*, Manchester: Manchester University Press.

Bourdieu, P., (1984) *Distinction*, London: Routledge.

Bourdieu, P., (1994) *Homo Academicus*, Cambridge: Polity.

Boyer, C., (1994) *The City of Collective Memory*, London, MIT Press.

Butler, T. and M. Rustin (eds), (1996) *Rising in the East? The Regeneration of East London* London: Lawrence and Wishart.

Castells, M., (1989) *The Information City*, Oxford: Basil Blackwell.

Cohen, P., (ed) (1996a) *For a Multicultural University*, London: CNER.

Cohen, P., (1996b) 'All White on the Night' in Butler and Rustin, *op. cit.*

Cohen, P., (1996c) 'Out of the Melting Pot into the Fire Next Time' in Westwood and Williams, *Imagining Cities*, London: Routledge.

Cohen, P., (1997a) 'Beyond the Community Romance', *Soundings* 5.

Cohen, P., (1997b) *Rethinking the Youth Question*, Basingstoke: Macmillan.

Harvey, D., (1988) *Social Justice and the City*, Oxford: Blackwell.

Hobbs, D., (1989) *Doing the Business*, Oxford: Oxford University Press.

Holland, R., (1990) *The Long Transition*, Basingstoke: Macmillan.

Hutton, W., (1995) *The State We're In*, London: Cape.

King, A. D. (ed), (1990) *Global Cities*, London: Routledge.

King, A. D. (ed), (1995) *Representing the City*, Basingstoke: Macmillan.

Kling, J., and P. Posner (eds), (1990) *Dilemmas of Activism*, Philadelphia: Temple Press.

Lave, J., (1991) *Situated Learning*, Cambridge: Cambridge University Press.

Massey, D., (1991) *Docklands*, London: Docklands Forum

Massey, D., (1994) *Space, Place and Gender*, Cambridge: Polity.

Melucci, A., (1989) *Nomads of the Present*, London: Radius.

Orwell, G., (1989) *The Road to Wigan Pier*, Harmondsworth: Penguin.

Sennett, R., (1994) *The Flesh and the Stone - the Body and the City in Western Civilization* London: Faber.

Sharma, V., *et al* (1997) *Dis-Orienting Rhythms*, London: Zed.

Sassen, S., (1995) 'Analytic Borderlands' in King.

Smyth, S., (1994) *Marketing the City*, London: Spon.

Soja, E., (1989) *Post Modern Geography*, London: Verso.

Willis, P., (1993) *Moving Culture*, Gulbenkian.

Wynne, D., (1993) *The Culture Industry*, Aldershot: Avebury.

Zukin, S., (1988) *Loft Living*, London: Radius.

Zukin, S., (1991) *Landscapes of Power*, Oxford: Oxford University Press.

NOTES

1. I have coined this term to highlight the hybrid character of these institutions positioned as they are between the elitist cultures of the 'old' universities, and the narrow vocationalism of the 'old' polytechnics. More positively the term also indicates the multiplication of different types of knowledge that are now potentially brought together within the curriculum of higher education.

2. This term was first used by Appadurai in his analysis of the role which ethnicity played in structuring the field of global information flows. It is used here to indicate the way cultural geographies of opportunity (or risk) are constructed through discourses of ethnicity.

The 'Eastern Promise' of New York and London

John Eade and Chris Mele

In this article John Eade and Chris Mele want to examine the similarities and differences between three areas - the East Village, Docklands and Spitalfields - located within two 'global cities' - New York and London.

Introduction

Although Sassen in her influential book, *The Global City*, chose New York, London and Tokyo as 'global cities' her emphasis on economic criteria (Sassen 1991, p5), and the role of global markets and the financial sector in particular, needs to be balanced with an analysis of the social, cultural and political processes operating within those global cities (see Robertson 1992 , Massey 1993, Lash and Urry 1994, Albrow 1996). Here we shall focus on the part played by the cultural reconstruction of urban localities in encouraging the economic, environmental and social changes which the term 'globalisation' attempts to describe. This cultural process is not simply determined by economic forces. Indeed, economic and environmental changes within New York and London are partly made possible by the changing images of place developed by specific individuals and organisations.

It is widely assumed that globalisation entails a homogenising process where national and local traditions are overwhelmed by global forces. However, we support those who point to the dynamic interplay between global and local which may have contradictory consequences, that is, an increasing indeterminacy in differentiating between people within particular localities (Albrow 1997) as well as the reassertion of 'traditional' solidarities including those based on the nation-state (Hall 1992, Harvey 1993). The interweaving of the global and the local means that local solidarities are being reshaped by forces which extend beyond metropolitan and national borders. The cultural reconstruction of place, therefore, plays a crucial role in encouraging global corporations and individuals to invest both their wealth and their time in the transformed localities of global cities like New York and London. These 'marginal places' are brought more closely into the centre of global business, ideologically as well as economically and environmentally.

Locality should, therefore, be seen 'as a fluid and relational space, constituted only in and through its relation to the global' (Morley and Robins 1995, p117) where distinctions between indigenous and extra-local cultural identities are increasingly blurred. Locality exists more as a 'dynamic medium' (Zukin 1992, p224) with several possible meanings attached to it by different actors rather than as a geographical site with a single socio-spatial identity (O'Byrne 1997). The fluidity of locale(s) may best be understood as several, potentially overlapping layers or 'scapes' which are dimensions of global flows. The particularities of place, such as the networks of residents and visitors, the level of corporate financial involvement or the images and representations associated with it vary not only between locales but within individual locales. A locality's architecture, streetscape and landmarks, for example, give rise to multiple interpretations and meanings conferred not only by local residents but also by corporate actors and real estate developers. Individuals navigate a variety of scapes or 'imagined worlds' which are 'constituted by the historically situated imaginations of persons and groups around the globe' (Appadurai, pp296-7). These scapes are not just individual constructs, therefore, nor are they detached from processes of power and inequality since through these 'imagined worlds' people 'can contest and even subvert' those constructed (physically and imaginatively) by officials and entrepreneurs (*Ibid*, p297).

Such is the wider sociological context for the ensuing investigation of recent efforts at urban restructuring which involve an ideological reconstruction of local images of place as well as political struggles over these changing images and the uses of community space . While issues of identity and redevelopment have long been contested in these locales we shall demonstrate how global processes during the 1980s and 1990s have not only reconfigured the terms of engagement between people but have also provided novel opportunities and constraints for the actions of both residents and developers. Although we point to the similarities between the localities in these two global cities, we shall also describe the significant differences in the ways in which local/global processes interweave as different social actors and economic sectors within each country play their distinctive parts.

Lineages of the working class

East Village, Docklands and Spitalfields played significant roles in the process of world-city building in the first half of this century. Their histories provide a well-spring of material on immigrant life, work, the built environment, ethnic and working-class cultures, and political activism. They were dormitories of the work force for the growing industrial economies. Tower Hamlets and other areas of the East End provided a home for Irish dock workers who laboured at the nearby Port of London (Smith 1932). East Europeans supplied the labour for the sweated garment industries in both cities (Shah 1975, Lin 1994). Following World War Two, the flow of peoples from the southern hemisphere and former colonial outposts toiled in firms which faced a shortage of low-wage workers. By the 1970s, Chinese, Puerto Rican, and later Mexicans in the Lower East Side (Mele 1994) as well as Bangladeshi and Turkish Cypriots in the East End (Eade 1989) worked in the much diminished garment and light manufacturing industries and faced a lifestyle much different than that of the previous immigrant cohorts.

Each district also contributed to the cultural fabric of its respective city. A strong literary heritage reflects the life and times of the various immigrant groups. In London, the East End was home to the Yiddish poet A. N. Stencl and writer Morris Winchevsky (Fishman 1985). The Lower East Side was the inspiration for Abraham Cahan's 1917 novel, *The Rise of David Levinsky*. In the post-war era, the Nuyorican Poets' Cafe was the site of creativity centred around the struggles of Puerto Ricans for independence from the US and the experience of adjustment in the Lower East Side. Samuel Selvon's *The Lonely Londoners* (1956) captured the hopes and fears of West Indians in London. These metropolitan locales also share similar social histories realised in the development and uses of the built environment. Cheek-by-jowl with rundown and substandard housing are fine examples of architecture and landscape that have been 'culturally recycled' with each successive wave of new inhabitants.

The near constant flows of diverse ethnic groups into each district is visible in the landscape. In Tower Hamlets' Spitalfields ward the Huguenot Church built in 1744 at the end of Fournier Street served as an Orthodox Synagogue at the turn of the nineteenth century and is currently used as a mosque. Likewise, former synagogues in the East Village now function as Latino Pentecostal *iglesia* (churches). Finally, strong lineages of political activism around issues of housing, the workplace and ethnic rights exist in both areas. Eastern Europeans, and especially Jewish immigrants, played a significant role in the development of socialist politics in the US and the UK (Fishman 1975). Collective action has historically reflected the position of the communities and their residents in relation to industrialisation, immigration and, in the post-war period, economic restructuring.

Culture and subversion in the East Village

In the summer of 1996, the *New York Times* declared the East Village the cultural capital of the United States. That determination was based on the recent prolific outpouring of cultural events and products from the area, including international fashion and music trends, the growth of media-based arts and the mainstream success of Rent, a Broadway musical that chronicles the lives of young adult misanthropes living amidst homelessness and squatting in the East Village. Six years earlier, most media attention was devoted to the moratorium on the neighbourhood's 'comeback', brought on by a spate of episodes of urban unrest and a downturn in the Manhattan real estate market. The emergence of the East Village as cultural capital is a result of its position within the global symbolic economy.

For most of the post-World War Two era, real estate development efforts mounted by private developers in co-ordination with the state sought to eradicate the area's overlapping working-class, low-income and counter-cultural identities. In an effort to disassociate the northern area from the stigmata of the larger Lower East Side, the real estate industry dubbed it the 'East Village' - an ancillary residential district to the more established and middle-class West Village. Although redevelopment ventures failed as the community suffered decline in the 1970s, the appellation remained. Today, the East Village contains a poly-centred population of activists, immigrants, artists and professionals where notions of community identity are fractured along an axis of the meaning of place which have been generated by local residents, global investors and real estate developers.

In the East Village during the 1980s real estate developers, bolstered by state reinvestment incentives, displaced scores of low-income and minority residents in an effort to create another residential neighbourhood designed to house middle- and upper-class professionals. Although significant levels of reinvestment occurred throughout the decade, the developers' efforts to replace the area's bohemian and downtown qualities with an upscale environment largely failed due to a combination of a bottomed-out luxury housing market and local resistance to gentrification (Mele 1994). During the 1990s, redevelopment has taken a different track as the strategy of eliminating the community's tradition of political, artistic and social resistance and subversion was abandoned and replaced by efforts to co-opt it (Mele 1996). The symbolism and lore of previous bouts of unrest triggered by homeless and squatter evictions, but indicative of a larger community struggle against displacement and gentrification, have provided the basis for the extra-local or global identity of exoticism and insurgency. For activists and participants in the area's 'indigenous' political culture, the political events surrounding Tompkins Square Park and other key sites were in response to the colonization of the neighbourhood by real estate developers. The representation of counter-culture, however, contributes to the area's packaging in film, music, theatre, writing and fashion (Smith 1996, pp3-29).

Since the late nineteenth century many of the alternative and innovative trends and movements in American art, literature, music and other entertainment forms were directly founded within the East Village (and the greater Lower East Side). Despite differences between these many movements - the diverse ethnic and religious forms, radical socialism, the beatniks, hippies, anarchists and squatters - all have shared a sense of purposeful opposition to mainstream and commodified culture and a reverence and desire to contribute to the legacy of cultural and political resistance which continues within this space. The historic diversity of the ethnic, racial and class composition of the East Village has been matched by a wealth of experimentation in art, music and writing that have questioned or countered dominant and mainsteam forms of culture. Previous genres associated with the East Village since the 1950s are the Abstract Expressionism of De Kooning and Johns, the writings of Ginsberg, Kerouac and Burroughs, and the Puerto Rican writers of the Nuyorican Poets' Cafe.

Recent changes at the global level in the access and availability of information and entertainment have elevated the status of the East Village as a counter-cultural enclave where future and profitable trends could be 'discovered' by the established corporate entertainment world (Mele 1996). During the 1980s local art galleries which showcased downtown artists such as Basquiat, Haring and Scharf purposefully marketed the 'underground art scene' in national and international venues. Political art - such as graffiti predicting doom for landlords and yuppies - which emerged during the unrest of the 1980s has been shown in galleries and reproduced in international art magazines.

Although many of the galleries have since closed, their presence contributed to the commodification of downtown culture or 'East Village genre' (Deutsche and Ryan 1984). This genre also includes experimentation in popular music. Initially the club, CPGB's, existed as a local venue for unpolished and undiscovered punk and then, during the late 1970s and early 1980s, as a venue for new wave bands. Although CPGB's remains a dark, uninviting club which continues to feature innovative performances, it is also part of a circuit of neighbourhood underground clubs frequented by talent scouts from specialised alternative music divisions of multi-national recording companies.

Elements of local gay culture have also migrated beyond the confines of the East Village. Within New York gay culture the East Village has provided an alternative to the West Village, post-Stonewall stereotype of a white, middle-class and accommodating gay lifestyle. The advent of the AIDS epidemic during the 1980s and the militant response to government inaction to the crisis contributed to the rise of a younger, more vocal and inclusive 'queer culture', much of it centred in East Village bars and clubs. Yearly events such as Wigstock, a mix of drag and political performances which were once held in Tompkins Square Park, have been popularised. The event grew so popular that it relocated to large venues in other areas of the city and has since been produced as a motion picture. During the early 1980s two night clubs, the Pyramid club on Avenue A and BoyBar on St. Mark's Place, were forums for an innovative 'East Village drag-transvestitism' which purposefully rejected celebrity-mimicry and realism. Performers were personalities in themselves and shows were performance art pieces which integrated issues of politics, race and sexuality into entertainment. The East Village drag scene provided an early venue for RuPaul, the six foot plus African-American drag singer/ perfomer who glamorised and mainstreamed drag culture on American and European television and radio.

The commodification of the off-beat or bohemian character of the East Village has had important ramifications for community identity. In the packaging of local culture for a global consumer niche market, corporate and sanitised images of locality come into conflict with everyday community meaning and identity conferred by residents. In the representational landscape of the East Village, all images and symbols selected are organised and presented to accentuate the experience of consumption.Thus the homeless, the squatters, the drug addicts and drug sellers are bit players and the abandoned buildings and trash-strewn lots are sets - they become objects and symbols disembedded and reassembled to create a artificial landscape of 'downtown' familiar not in the immediate experience of the East Village, but globally as an aesthetic or style related to cultural products of music, fiction, fashion and art. That manufactured identity of downtown aesthetic is spatialised in the development of retail shops, eateries, and bars, as well as in the larger streetscape. Here graffiti, political posters and other visual images of discontent are signage of the downtown aesthetic. A single set of economic, cultural and social symbols - such as landscape and architecture, local politics and drug culture, community lore and customs, relations between ethnicities and races - become sources for the construction of a synthetic identity of place. Through appropriation of local cultural forms, a synthetic sense of place is constructed around particular elements of real places that are disembedded to create a 'global localism' (Castells 1996).

New construction in the East Village reflects the eclectic social and cultural composition of the East Village and incorporates the somewhat harsh realities of everyday living with the commodified and illusory synthetic identity of the 'bohemian lifestyle'. Red Square, a recently constructed high-rent apartment building, is situated deep in the less developed and poorer area of the East Village. The architecture is purposefully non-confrontational and attempts to blend into the environment of barren tenements and trash-strewn streets. A non-working clock face with randomly arranged numerals adorns the tower atop the thirteen storey building. Views from the well-appointed apartments range from Wall Street, to the midtown skyline or the adjacent landscape of five and six storey tenements and empty lots. Urban sculptures constructed from scrap-metal in the vein of the now-defunct Rivington School (in the Lower East Side) are fastened to the buildings cornices. Red Square's tenants are young, well-educated and employed in the city's art, fashion, design, publishing or music industries. They were drawn to Red Square because, as one resident said: 'it is playful, which is what the East Village is all about'. Red Square and a handful of other rental and condominium buildings profit from combining the culture of downtown and the amenities of luxury buildings. Although these rental and condominium buildings were novel cases of marketing to combine two extreme appeals - the luxury within and the worn urban landscape outside - they symbolise a growing trend among developers to fashion housing units for small market niches of consumers. Real estate developers have been successful in spatialising the cultural image of the East Village, embracing its most profitable elements and discarding others.

Developers' efforts to fuse spaces of representation or imagination (synthetic identity) with material spatial practices (new forms of development) have reconfigured expressions of resistance by locals to neighbourhood change. A prime example is the unusual co-existence of gentrification and functioning neighborhood drug enclaves. In the midst of intensive neighbourhood redevelopment, pockets of the East Village continue to house drug distribution markets, especially the dealing of heroin and cocaine. Dense and complex social networks of low-income residents coupled their state rent-regulated status and participation in the informal economy of drug sales to construct elaborate 'safe zones' which present an effective, yet disorganised (and unanticipated), resistance to the emptying out of buildings and entire blocks of residents. The community life of these blocks is stable. Residential displacement and turnover remain minimal and most tenants have lived on these blocks since birth or since their arrival from Puerto Rico in the early 1960s. The drug trade and its somewhat impermeable social network has unintentionally acted as a barrier to displacement pressures. In a few instances, partial revenues from drug dealing have been funnelled into building maintenance and upkeep and block-level community organisations . Within these same blocks, an increase in newcomers drawn to both cheap rents and the media-influenced repute of the East Village has occurred. Thus within the scale of single block, multiple and conflicting community identities overlap and the social and cultural defiance mounted by threatened residents is, at once, an act of resistance to urban change and a source of content for the re-imaging of the East Village for high end consumption. Drug culture, graffiti, demonstrations, music, poetry and other forms of passive and active resistance are expressions of discontent and the basis of a commodified East Village aesthetic.

Appropriating difference: Docklands and Spitalfields

Although we have already outlined a variety of similarities between the East Village, Docklands and Spitalfields we must resist the temptation to overstate those likenesses since the East End of London has shown nothing like the cultural dynamism evident in the East Village during the 1980s and 1990s. Similar strategies of co-opting local traditions of resistance and subversion have been pursued to create a powerful image of a 'safe' exoticism and insurgency but in East London those strategies have not involved the city's cultural industry to any significant degree. The urban heritage of these London localities have indeed been reconfigured through a dynamic interplay between local and global forces but through ways which involve actors outside the cultural sectors of music, fiction, fashion and art.

DOCKLANDS

The concept of Docklands is largely a recent construction designed to replace or reinterpret older names associated with working-class communities (the Isle of Dogs, Shadwell, Wapping, Limehouse, Cubitt Town). The promotion of Docklands was intimately bound up with the creation of the London

Docklands Development Corporation (LDDC) and was intended to describe an area far beyond Tower Hamlets; into the Royal Docks of Newham and the Surrey Docks across the river in Rotherhithe (see Brownhill 1990, Fainstein 1994, pp189-217). The concept and image of 'Docklands' was developed by the LDDC in order to promote a symbolic unity out of the highly disparate range of localities as part of its strategy of attracting outside investment and presenting a rival magnet to the City of London.

To provide Docklands with a new identity, much use was made of the River Thames, water and anything associated with docks - water sports, ships and barges, the structures of the docks, the warehouses and the industrial machinery. The contribution of working-class people to the localities which were radically transformed under the aegis of the LDDC was seldom acknowledged in the publicity material generated during the 1980s, although some recompense was made by the Visitors' Centre near Canary Wharf in the heart of the Tower Hamlets' area of Docklands.

The re-imaging of the localities within the Docklands wards in southern Tower Hamlets primarily entailed the forging of a link between a nostalgic version of local heritage and the new developments which were designed for the banking and finance houses, high tech businesses and the enterprises which serviced those national and global operations. The image of a transformed Docklands played a crucial role in attracting settlers from Britain's 'new service class' as well as overseas staff employed by the multi-national corporations and global property investors. These were the kinds of people whom estate agents sought to interest in the new housing and the refurbished warehouses around the old St Katharine's, London, Shadwell, West Indies and Millwall docks.

An illustration of the way in which 'Docklands' was imaged is provided by a 1980s London Docklands Tours leaflet:

> The vast regeneration now roaring ahead in London Docklands is the most widely known inner-city development story in Europe. Everyone knows of it or has read of it, yet few have more than a vague idea of what is happening in this this enormous 8.5 square mile area down river from Tower Bridge.
>
> Within walking distance of London's historic financial centre the unique riverside areas of Wapping, Limehouse, Rotherhithe and the Isle of Dogs, the lingering aroma of the now disused spice warehouses sitting alongside spectacular new housing provides a unique setting for visitors to London's famous Docklands.

In this picture of a new world - Docklands - the past is still conjured up, but it is a nostalgic heritage associated with buildings which stored the exotic spices brought by Britain's ocean-going cargo ships. The sailors who worked in those ships and the dock workers whose descendants still remained in Docklands are left out of this account . To the visitor and the intrigued investor the emphasis was on the creation of a new physical and social environment where the remnants of the old industrial order played a part mainly in a nostalgic and exotic version of nineteenth century London.

The juxtaposition of wealthy newcomers and their poorer neighbours in Docklands was a source of discordance which nostalgic constructions of a local urban heritage sought to resolve. When it came to selling the new property to global investors, estate agents could pursue several strategies to resolve the dissonance created by the sharp social and economic differences between the newcomers and their future working class neighbours. One strategy was to construct an image of an authentic friendly East Ender as one agent explained:

> we encourage people to go locally and we give people lists of places to go and the names of publicans and where they can eat...I love the East Enders. They're absolutely great. They're very friendly. They're very like the North of England people...I lived in the North for several years. The typical Londoner, to me, is not friendly. Nobody speaks to you on the tube or bus. (quoted in Eade 1997, p133)

This construction of a friendly local avoided a long history of racialised conflict where some white residents at least had intimidated Bangladeshi settlers in particular (see Cohen 1996). Estate agents were well aware of this continuing racial tension and some pursued another strategy in their bid to attract Pacific Rim investors to Docklands. Parallels could be drawn with the gleaming waterfront developments of Hong Kong and Singapore:

> The Orientals: the Far Easterners, Malaysians, Singaporeans, Hong Kongese are most receptive to Docklands as an idea because they have seen [similar developments in their own countries]. Since the rejuvenation of their countries they can relate to anything modern. Then you have some cultural reasons for wanting to be on water and being high up. But anything old is frowned upon. (*Ibid*, p134)

Here the image of a nostalgic local heritage and an awareness of continuing racial tension are carefully set aside for a picture of a totally new world similar to urban landscapes elsewhere. However, the power of cultural traditions is still acknowledged even though the focus in now on the traditions of the oriental investors. These wealthy newcomers would still be seen as alien to racist white residents but some protection could be provided by the defences of their 'state of the art' apartment blocks and by another strategy - avoidance - which one estate agent encouraged all prospective buyers to adopt:

> When I give people a map I say: 'These are the the areas [to avoid] and I 'X' off the council [housing] areas because they are not going to buy there anyway so they don't want to wander around these places. (*Ibid*, p133)

In this section on Docklands we have concentrated upon the role played by the LDDC and estate agents in constructing a new image for the southern wards of Tower Hamlets. We have described the attempts by powerful institutions and social actors to incorporate nostalgic, exotic elements of a local past which conveniently ignored the discordant presence of class and racial division. As we have already seen in the East Village of New York, this cultural reconstruction of urban locality produced synthetic spatial identities which could be combined with the material spatial practices of urban development. However, developers in this area of New York tried to symbolically embrace rather than ignore social and cultural differences between locals and newcomers. They encouraged the emergence of new 'anarchist' cafes, expensive fashion boutiques specialising in an aesthetic of recycled clothing, and well-appointed apartment buildings which integrated visual elements of the neighbouhood's marginalised subcultures. This strategy challenged both the collective identity and the forms of resistance generated by Puerto Ricans and other poorer locals.

The developers in Docklands pursued a different strategy in the context of a very different social and cultural environment. This area of London did not experience the kinds of vigorous artistic developments and counter-cultural assertions evident in East Village. However, the development of Docklands presented a similar challenge to its working class residents. They also sought to resist attempts to incorporate them within a nostalgic version of urban heritage through the generation of local history projects, for example, and asserted their contemporary presence in the rapidly changing Docklands through their political and community organisations. To illuminate in more detail how local organisations sought to contest the re-imaging of their neighbourhoods through nostalgic versions of the past we will now move away from Docklands to Spitalfields on Tower Hamlets' western border with the City of London.

SPITALFIELDS

Unlike Docklands the identity of Spitalfields was not a recent creation nor were large parts of the ward so visibly affected by the settlement of wealthy newcomers. However, the movement of offices and specialist businesses from the City of London had slowly changed the character of the streets directly abutting the City boundary while the gradual gentrification of the eighteenth century houses in the central conservation area of Spitalfields also entailed the settlement of wealthy residents who were in some cases lively promoters of the area's aesthetic redevelopment. Spitalfields was also home to a Bangladeshi community which constituted over 60 per cent of the ward's population by 1991 (Eade 1997, p139). This community dominated the local garment industry, restaurants, cafes and small shops as well as its political and community activities.

The re-imaging of this locality by developers had to contend with repeated counter-assertions from Bangladeshi and non-Bangladeshi activists who emphasised the working-class and multi-cultural character of Spitalfields (see Eade 1989, 1996, Forman 1989, Fainstein 1994, Jacobs 1996). However, the struggles around the cultural construction of place did not simply involve a straightforward process of resistance by locals against powerful developers. Alliances between political and community activists were always tenuous given the different political and cultural understandings which they pursued. Developers sometimes wished to encourage local participation in their schemes, but did not appreciate the diverse ways in which an innovation could be interpreted by local residents.

Truman's Brewery: Site of the former Music Hall (now the Vibe Bar) © John Eade

An early 1990s redevelopment along Brick Lane - the symbolic and material core of Bangladeshi Spitalfields - provided an illustration of the complex diversity of interpretations which a new development both created and encouraged. A major corporation, Grand Metropolitan, decided to close its historic Truman's Brewery and to redevelop part of the brewery's eighteenth century buildings as a tourist attraction. Grand Met joined local organisations and borough council representatives to establish the East End Trust and provided the Trust with office space within the old brewery. As well as encouraging 'good' Bangladeshi restaurants in the area, the Trust also sought to build on Spitalfields' East End past by establishing the Brick Lane Music Hall in the old brewery.

The East End Trust wished to attract tourists and Londoners who wanted a 'fun evening out' involving a meal and entertainment in a historic setting. The new venture, therefore, tried to invoke the music halls of Victorian and Edwardian London through language and images which echoed a 1970s television music hall series, 'The Good Old Days'. In the alliterative language which became the trademark of the Master of Ceremonies in the television programme an East End Trust's publicity leaflet announced that:

> An evening of rare rapport and sophisticated sauciness awaits discerning pleasure seekers...
> Escape from reality into a world of abandoned frivolity, scrumptious suppers and bargain beverages.
> Each week will bring named artists at prices only we can afford, complementing the musical director, our master of ceremonies, a bewitching bevvy of beauties - and the legendary Dockyard Doris.
> Dine before the show. A scrumptious three-course dinner served each evening. Latkas a speciality. (quoted in Eade 1997, p136)

The leaflet conjures up an urban past when different classes rubbed shoulders in an atmosphere of raunchy fun encouraged by Dockyard Doris, a drag act. However, representatives of the Great London Mosque which also occupied an eighteenth century building on Brick Lane were scandalised by the entertainment on offer. While local political activists did not necessarily share the Islamic concerns of the mosque's representatives, some of them expressed their hostitlity to the way in which the locality was being used as a resource by people who appeared to be uninterested in engaging with the multicultural diversity of contemporary Spitalfields. Although the criticisms by religious and political leaders failed to deter the new venture the conflict aroused by the music hall demonstrated the challenge which local leaders could mount and the alliances which could be generated

Brick Lane Mosque, Spitalfields, looking west down Fournier Street © John Eade

between these leaders despite their ideological differences.

The East End Trust's presentation of the Brick Lane music hall revealed once more the attempt by developers to promote a nostalgic version of an urban past which ignored the unsettling presence of those beyond the boundaries of their version of a safe, happy place. As in Docklands their image of locality was designed to attract tourists and other outsiders who could not fail to see the Bangladeshi impact on this area of London but who could also look past the complicated and diverse present to a homely, vanished world where late nineteenth century East European Jewish settlement could be represented by cuisine - the potato cake or 'latkas, a speciality'.

Spitalfields had not attracted the kinds of overseas investors and global corporations which had entered Docklands, but the nostalgic image which was represented in the Brick Lane Music Hall publicity fitted into a vision of the 'East End' promoted around the world by film, television, novels and documentaries (see Schwarz 1991). Even violence could be safely incorporated into this nostalgic image as the contemporary use of the 1880s Jack the Ripper mystery by developers indicates. One local estate agent explained the continuing power of this aspect of local heritage to overseas visitors:

> You've got to keep a bit of the original Jack the Ripper territory because, obviously, that's a great pulling point for the tourists around here. It was around Spitalfields that the supposed murders took place...So you've got to keep that otherwise you'll lose what was the city, the East End of London, and what people remember of it. If you talk to Americans all they think of is: 'Have you got the fog?' and 'Where's Jack the Ripper?' and 'Isn't this quaint?' and they're the sort of people that want to see these Georgian buildings. (quoted in Eade 1997, p135)

Again local activists challenged the ways in which commercial interests exploited the Jack the Ripper myth in Spitalfields and their most successful campaign so far involved the changing of the name of a local public house from Jack the Ripper to the Ten Bells. Even so the evening walking tours around 'Jack the Ripper country' in Spitalfields remained popular attracting the tourist looking for an 'authentic', 'alternative' experience beyond the honeypots of the Tower of London, Tower Bridge and St Katharine's Dock to the south.

Local political and community activists had usually criticised these attempts by private businesses to market Spitalfields to the outside world. Local resistance to moves by major City of London property companies to redevelop substantial areas of west and central Spitalfields were strengthened by the collapse of the property market in 1991-2. However, Spitalfields' proximity to the City of London and the tourist area around the Tower of the London meant that politicians, planners and private companies continued to look for ways to exploit the economic potential of this and neighbouring western wards. That potential has been recently enhanced by the revival of the property market across London encouraging those who wanted to redevelop Spitalfields in ways which would actually gain the support of local residents.

A current example of the attempt to ally the interests of residents, public officials and private business is provided by the '"Rich Mix Centre" for London' proposal. The Centre is intended to occupy a former warehouse in central Spitalfields. If the proposal succeeds, this Moorish-style building would be redesigned to house a 'Virtual Reality' hall and archive celebrating London's multi-cultural diversity as well as food, craft and design halls. The Centre would be linked to other places of multicultural significance, namely the Fournier Street conservation area, the Brick Lane mosque and Christ's Church, Spitalfields designed by Sir Christopher Wren's famous pupil, Nicholas Hawksmoor.

Throughout the document submitted to the Millennium Commission

Site of proposed Rich Mix centre © John Eade

in a bid for funding the authors' regard for local heritage is combined with a desire to establish the venture as both a metropolitan and national centre. There is also a clear understanding of London's role 'as a world city' and the intimate link between its multicultural character and global movement of people and capital:

> As cities, regions and nations will increasingly be made up of diverse mixes of population groups it is imperative to foster positively the new hybrid cosmopolitanism that is emerging in contemporary metropolitan life. This will become increasingly important in the context of globalisation, the rapid movement of capital and mass migration of people triggered by the new world production order. (*Submission to Millennium Commission*, p5)

Interestingly, the document proceeds to compare London with New York as the world's two most cosmopolitan cities. London's ethnic diversity links the city 'to all corners of the globe' and, quoting another prospectus, provides '"the rich mix of skills, talents and traditions which will help us to underpin the city's cultural and economic development in the next century" (London Pride Prospectus)' (*Ibid.*).

Until the summer of 1997 consultation over the Rich Mix proposal had largely involved political and community representatives, council officials and consultants across the city as well as the 'local Banglatown Working Party, consisting of business representatives and other stakeholders in the area' (*Ibid*, p7). A much wider net was to be cast during the summer while negotiations were completed with the Millennium Commission. The proposal document tries to attract local support by describing the economic, educational and environmental benefits but the authors want to balance local interests with wider concerns. They are pursuing a 'holistic approach' which

> aims to find ways of balancing the differing needs and aspirations of local, London wide and UK communities, and will provide opportunities for international links with the historic homes of immigrant groups and institutions. (*Ibid.*)

The strategy of building alliances between politicians, community activists, council officials and local businesses has been promoted by a Labour Party which returned to power in the 1994 council elections after eight years in opposition. Labour councillors representing Spitalfields and neighbouring wards found themselves in a position where they could no longer engage in pure resistance to the development plans of council officials and investors. The themes of multiculturalism and local community which the left-wing Labour activists espoused to oppose development plans before 1994 (see Woodward 1993, Jacobs 1996) are now being used to establish an alliance with Bangladeshi businessmen who had promoted Brick Lane as the heart of a 'Banglatown' thereby trading

> on an essentialised notion of their culture as a component part of a broader plan to control redevelopment in their favour: acquire land, ensure social amenity and establish opportunities for Bengali youths to enter the 'City' workforce. (Jacobs 1996, p100)

Yet this alliance will be difficult to sustain given not only the different interests among Bangladeshi and non-Bangladeshi community groups and commercial concerns, but also the strains of linking those diverse interests to the cultural and business entrepreneurs across London, the nation and overseas.

From our perspective the most interesting aspect of the Rich Mix Centre proposal is its awareness of the economic potential of cultural creativity in a global context. The venture suggests that this part of London could attract the talents of those within the media and the arts in ways which parallel what has been happening in New York's East Village. Instead of re-imaging the locality in terms of nostalgic, exotic verisions of a local past Spitalfields could be presented as part of the city's contemporary hip image. Page five of the prospectus approvingly quotes, for example, a purple passage from *Newsweek* describing this state of the art image:

> London is a hip compromise between the non-stop newness of Los Angeles and the aspic-preserved beauty of Paris - sharpened to New York's edge. In short, this is the coolest city of the planet. (*Newsweek*, November 4, 1996)

Clearly the *Newsweek* journalist was not referring to the dystopic aspects of inner city London evident within a stone's throw of the proposed Rich Mix Centre!

Conclusion

We began this article with the claim that global/local processes are characterised by multiple, richly complex and, sometimes, conflicting layers of interaction between community and global realms of political, economic and economic life. We have attempted to ground this assertion in a description of contemporary urban development in three areas of New York and London. In these areas the local idiosyncracies of community identity and urban heritage were no longer hindrances to redevelopment, but served as sources of images and symbols selectively represented to advance the physical redevelopment of the localities.

The ways in which these particular industries and social actors operated clearly varied between New York and London, of course. The *content* of the social, economic, cultural and political forces at work in each area was sometimes strikingly different and the role of the cultural industry in the East Village contrasted sharply with the commercial interests at work in Docklands and Spitalfields - the recent Rich Mix Centre initiative notwithstanding. Yet all three areas were affected by the same *process* where non-local (or global) representations of place promoted the physical redevelopment of local communities.

The cultural reconstruction of locality in these three localities varied in content as local histories were worked on and different social actors pursued their particular strategies. Yet the effect was similar : the overlapping of several images of place and the increasing fluidity of locality associated with the interweaving of the interests of global corporations and individual investors, national and metropolitan agencies, wealthy newcomers and working-class residents.

The importance of cultural representation in shaping not only the ways in which localities were perceived, but also how they were physically redeveloped presents a major challenge to the strategies and goals of local political and community movements which mobilise against community redevelopment. Although global marketing and representations of previously marginal places (marginal to global investors!) purposefully conceal or fail to recognise the conflicts of class, race and ethnicity, such inequalities remain the basis for local social action. At the same time, however, local expressions of discontent are problematised by a global economy which incorporates (rather than eliminates) historic and contemporary symbols of resistance. In redefining and manipulating local images, symbols and cultural products for global consumption new opportunities have been created for developers to restructure place.

Traditional repertoires of community resistance to urban change are often unsuitable against this process of image construction which accompanies the economic and environmental transformation of these three metropolitan areas. Moreover, the agents or sources of globalisation do not exist as easily identifiable protagonists. This dual fracturing of agents and process makes it difficult for local activists to resist and to agree on their common enemies. Small victories may be won and temporary alliances may be forged, as we have seen in Spitalfields, but resistance is weakened by the differing ideological interests of local activists and the invention of multiple and overlapping identities codified by the state (conservation areas, enterprise zones etc) and by developers.

Repertoires and discourses of resistance need to both reflect and address global processes, therefore, as well as appreciate their impact upon particular local interests and environments. The current bid for a Rich Mix Centre in Spitalfields suggests that local politicians and community activists understand the need to rethink the strategy of outright opposition to non-local forces. They understand this particular locality's relationship to London as a global city and to the 'new world production order'. In the process they are also engaging in the re-imaging of Spitalfields whereby the global and the local interweave and new images of the locality are created. Despite the superficial similarities between Spitalfields and the East Village which are generated by these developments, crucial differences remain because of the different mixture of social actors and institutions operating within the two neighbourhoods. Docklands also remains significantly different from the other two localities as its development is shaped by the interweaving and sometimes colliding of global investors and their investments, the 'new service class' and a racialised working class.

Individual understandings of these three localities are crucially shaped by the overlapping layers of meanings and diverse images of place generated by the interplay of global and local flows of people, capital and information.

They have to negotiate a complex world of 'global localism' where there is no pure opposition between the global and the local and no simple process of global cultural homogenisation. There are signs that some local activists and officials are aware of the implications which this complexity for the creation of what Massey (1993) calls a 'progressive sense of place'. Only time will tell how far this awareness will extend to other people and to what extent it will be challenged by rival versions of 'progress' .

The authors wish to acknowledge the helpful advice and support provided by Garry Marvin, Darren O'Byrne, Anne Kershen and Tim Butler.

REFERENCES

Albrow, M., (1996) *The Global Age*, Cambridge: Polity Press.

Albrow, M., (1997) 'Travelling beyond Local Cultures: Socioscapes in a Global in City' in Eade, J. (ed), *Living the Global City: Globalization as Local Process*, London and New York: Routledge.

Appadurai, A., (1990) 'Disjuncture and Difference in the Global Cultural Economy', *Theory, Culture and Society*, Volume 7, pp 295-310.

Brownhill, S. , *Developing London's Docklands: Another Great Planning Disaster?*, P. Chapman, London.

Castells, M., (1996) *The Rise of the Network Society*,Cambridge, Mass: Blackwell.

Cohen, P., (1996) 'All White on the Night? Narratives of Nativism on the Isle of Dogs' in T. Butler and M. Rustin (eds), *Rising in the East: The Regeneration of East London*, London: Lawrence and Wishart, pp170-196.

Deutsche, R. and C. Ryan, (1984) 'The Fine Art of Gentrification', *October*, Volume 31, pp 91-111.

Eade, J., (1989) *The Politics of Community: The Bangladeshi Community in East London*, Aldershot: Avebury.

Eade, J., (1996) 'Nationalism, Community and the Islamization of Space in London' in B. Metcalf (ed), *Making Muslim Space in North America and Europe*, Berkeley and and Los Angeles: University of California Press, pp 217-33.

Eade, J., (1997) 'Reconstructing Places: Changing Images of Locality in "Docklands" and Spitalfields' in J. Eade (ed.), *Living the Global City*, London and New York: Routledge, pp 127-45.

Fainstein, S., (1994) *The City Builders: Property, Politics and Planning in London and New York*, Cambridge, Mass: Blackwell.

Fishman, W., (1975) *East End Jewish Radicals 1875-1914*, London: Duckworth.

Fishman, W., (1985) 'Morris Winchevsky's London Yiddish Newspaper: One Hundred Years in Retrospect', *Oxford Centre for Postgraduate Hebrew Studies*.

Forman, C., (1989) *Spitalfields: A Battle for Land*, London: H. Shipman.

Hall, S., (1992) 'The Question of Cultural Identity' in S. Hall, D. Held and A. McGrew (eds), *Modernity and Its Futures*, Milton Keynes: Polity, Cambridge and Open University Press.

Harvey, D. , (1993) 'From Space to Place and Back Again: Reflections on the Condition of Postmodernity' in J. Bird *et al.* (eds) *Mapping the Futures: Local Cultures, Global Change,* London and New York: Routledge, pp3-29.

Jacobs, J., (1996) *Edge of Empire: Postcolonialism and the City*, London and New York: Routledge.

Lash, S. and Urry, J., (1994) *Economies of Signs and Space*, London and New York: Routledge.

Lin, J., (1994) 'The Changing Economy of the Lower East Side' in J. Abu-Lughod et al. (eds) *From Urban Village to East Village: The Battle for New York's Lower East Side,* Cambridge, Mass: Blackwell.

Massey, D., (1993) 'Power-Geometry and a Progressive Sense of Place' in J. Bird *et al* (eds), *Mapping the Futures: Local Cultures, Global Change*, London and New York: Routledge.

Mele, C., (1994) 'Neighborhood Burn-Out: Puerto Ricans at the End of the Queue' in J. Abu-Lughod *et al* (eds), *From Urban Village to East Village: The Battle for New York's Lower East Side*, Cambridge, Mass: Blackwell.

Mele, C., (1996) 'Changing Forms of Displacement in the East Village of New York', *Comparative Urban and Community Research*, Volume 5, pp69-94.

Morley, D. and Robins, K., (1995) *Spaces of Identity: Global Media, Electronic Landscapes and Cutural Boundaries*, London and New York: Routledge.

O'Byrne, D., (1997) 'Working-Class Culture: Local Community and Global Conditions' in J. Eade (ed) *Living the Global City: Globalization as Social Process*, London and New York: Routledge, pp 73-89.

Robertson, R., (1992) *Globalization*, London: Sage.

Sassen, S., (1991) *The Global City: New York, London, Tokyo*, Princeton, N.J: Princeton University Press.

Schwarz, W., (1991) 'Where Horses Shit a Hundred Sparrows Feed: 'Docklands' and East London during the Thatcher Years' in J. Corner and S. Harvey (eds), *Enterprise and Heritage: Crosscurrents of National Culture*, London and New York: Routledge, pp 76-92.

Shah, S., (1975) *Immigrants and Employment in the Clothing Industry: The Rag Trade in London's East End*, London: Runnymede Trust.

Smith, H. (ed), (1932) *The New Survey of London and Labour, Vol. 111 Survey of Social Conditions (1) The Eastern Area*, London: P. King.

Smith, N., (1996) *The New Urban Frontier: Gentrification and the Revanchist City*, London and New York: Routledge.

Woodward, R., (1993) 'One Place, Two Stories: Two Interpretations of Spitalfields in the Debate over its Redevelopment' in G. Kearns and C. Philo (eds), *Selling Places: The City as Cultural Capital, Past and Present*, Oxford and New York: Pergamon.

Zukin, S., (1992) 'Postmodern Urban Landscapes: Mapping Culture and Power' in S. Lash and J. Friedman (eds), *Modernity and Identity*, Cambridge, Mass: Blackwell.

Zukin, S., (1995) *The Culture of Cities*, Cambridge, Mass: Blackwell.

LPAC's[1] East London development focus

Martin Simmons and Abigail Warren

Martin Simmons and Abigail Warren argue the case for an East London focus.

Tim Butler's editorial in the first issue of *Rising East* asked questions about East London's relative underperformance and why east-west differences persist across London. Drew Stevenson's paper on structuring change set out five components of a holistic East London strategy aimed at improving its performance: economic, social, infrastructural, environmental and developmental. Anna Whyatt, identifying the key characteristics for a successful revival of the London Thames Gateway area, discussed how the area may gain competitive advantage for specific sectors of employment - generating activity for which it has potential. These pieces consistently advocate the importance of vision and strategy, both to raise people's aspirations and to establish East London's position in the regional geography of investment and development. This article seeks to add to that strategy-making LPAC's East London Development Focus (ELDF), which we believe to be an important planning concept to draw attention to this side of the capital, in this new era of proactive regionalism.

The growing policy concentration on the eastern side of London by central government this decade is in part, at least, a response to advice pressed on it by the regional planning organisations LPAC, representing the London planning authorities, and the South East Regional Planning Conference (SERPLAN), an organisation of those in the wider region including LPAC. Indeed, if we look back on why regional planning has revived this decade, recognition by central government of the necessity of redressing the imbalance between the buoyant west and the needy east is the most apparent reason. It was first referred to in planning guidance on the impact of the M25 extracted from a reluctant government in 1984

(DoE, 1988), given impetus in SERPLAN's identification of the East Thames Corridor between 1986 and 1990 (SERPLAN, 1990), after which Michael Heseltine was persuaded to take it over by his planning adviser Peter Hall, and then in the new and much improved Regional Planning Guidance for the South East (RPG 9, DoE 1994). This guidance was the formal expression of government policy to extend regeneration activity beyond Docklands to the East Thames Corridor. The guidance also established, uniquely for government, a sub-regional strategy in the form of the Thames Gateway (renaming the Corridor) Planning Framework, covering the area between the Lower Lea Valley and Deptford in East London out to the Thameside and Medway towns areas of north-west Kent (RPG9A, DoE, 1995).

LPAC took its role in the revival of strategic regional planning onwards in 1994 with the production of its Advice on new Strategic Planning Guidance for London, in the form of an advisory structure plan for the capital (LPAC, 1994). This started with a four-fold vision of London as a city combining a strong economy, an improving quality of life, opportunities for all and a sustainable future. Realisation of this vision requires a pan-London balance in social and economic development. Chapter 2 of LPAC's 1994 Advice provides a cross-London geographic structure to this end. This aims to realise a developmental balance across London, consolidating the more buoyant areas and regenerating the more needy parts. To some extent imbalances have an inner and outer dimension, but in developmental terms the differences between east and west London are the most apparent, with the largest areas of deprivation being in the inner east (see Figure 1 overleaf). Not only has east London suffered the most dramatic economic decline and loss of employment, it also presents by far the most extensive opportunities, in terms of resources of land and labour, of anywhere in the London region. London's continuing success as a world city requires the effective use of these resources, while the social cohesion essential to a sustainable metropolis requires the fulfilling realisation of its large human potential.

LPAC's experience has been that the main growth sectors of the London economy, to the extent that they are not based in the centre, prefer to locate to the west. A nexus of factors, some real, others perceived, explain this: closeness to the expanding Heathrow airport; better surface transport; access to a labour force more skilled in the occupations in demand; more attractive living environments. Most of the firms which have decentralised from London into the rest of the south-east have chosen the western side, usually into the arc between the A3 and the M1, often to car-based 'B1'

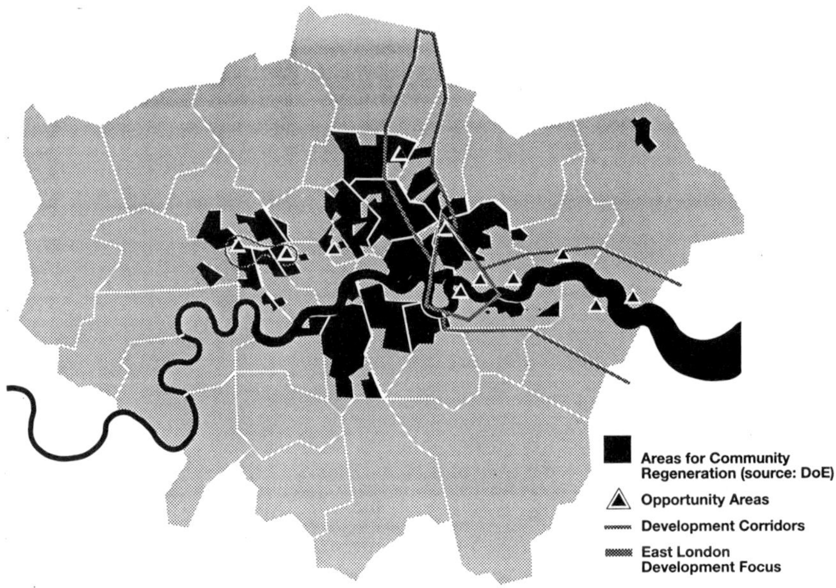

Figure 1: Regeneration and opportunity areas

business parks (Jones Lang Wooten, 1997).

Countering this business investment predilection in favour of the West is essential if the aims of regenerating East London are to succeed. Important measures are already in place: the Government's commitment through the Thames Gateway Planning Framework, the East London Lea Valley Objective 2 area (Figure 2) and the framework these provide for the various successful bids for Single Regeneration Budget and other project funding. However, LPAC believes, from its knowledge of the factors driving business location across the London region, that the investing community will need more persuasion to 'look east'. Our contribution is the ELDF.

Defining the East London development focus

So what is the ELDF? It is located where the southern end of the Lea Valley Objective 2 area overlaps with the London end of the Thames Gateway area (Figure 1). In addition to being the recipient of regeneration funding from the European structural funds and from the British government, this part of East London is the subject of much current and impending infrastructure

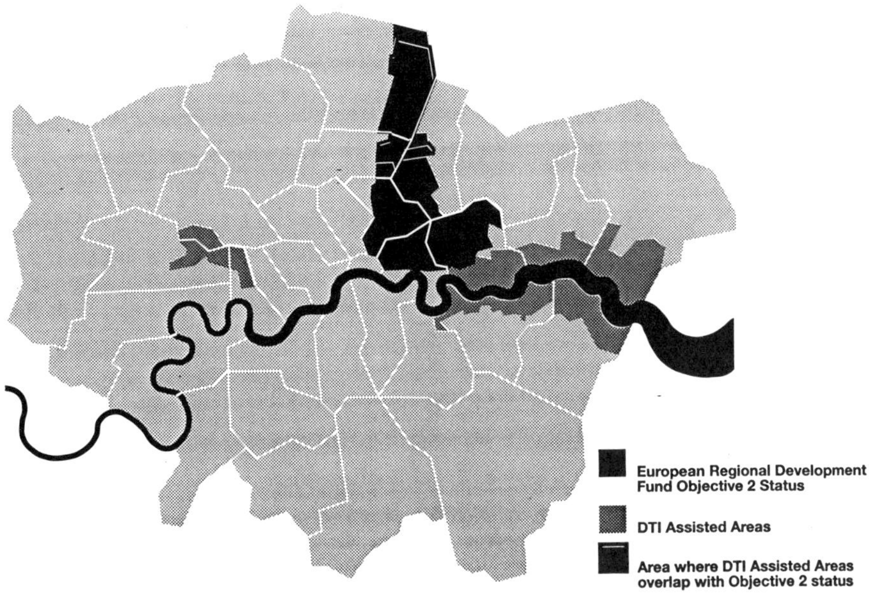

Figure 2: DTI Assisted Areas and Objective 2 Status

development. LPAC's concept relates these advantages to the greatest concentration of land development opportunity in East London. We believe that this would create a powerful synergy which can be used to promote the attractions of the area as a whole. It would give East London a powerful strategic tool to overcome the bias in favour of the West and counter the forces causing decentralisation of activities from inner London.

LPAC's Advice sees the ELDF in these terms:

> It is vital to the achievement of the Four-fold Vision, the Objectives regarding economic revival and urban regeneration, and to London's world city role and competitive future in Europe, that the capacity and resources available here are fully harnessed to realise a new and vibrant heart for East London. Together, this area can achieve a new multi-site commercial, higher education, research and technological innovation, exhibition, culture and leisure complex, to complement Central London (LPAC, 1994).

Key development locations in the focus

Let us examine the key components of the Focus (Figure 3).

Figure 3:
East London Development Focus development locations

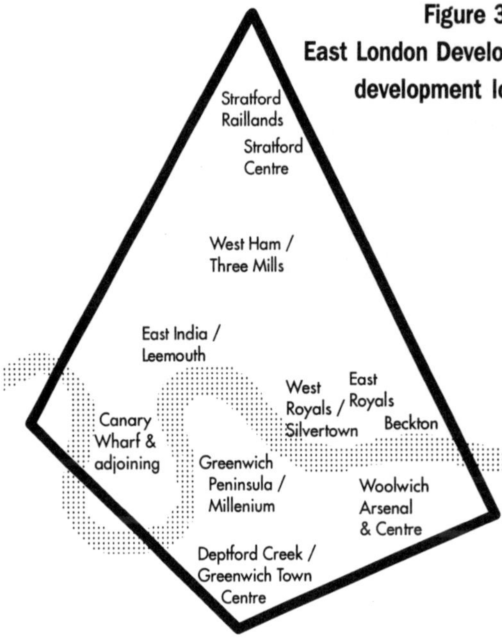

ISLE OF DOGS/CANARY WHARF

LPAC recognises the new 'Special Business District' at and around Canary Wharf as very significant in shifting the investment balance from west to east. It is therefore an integral part of the ELDF. While its benefit to surrounding communities has been disappointing, its contribution to the synergy to be created between development in the Focus will be considerable in 'critical mass' terms, given its visual prominence, its transport links and bearing in mind that considerable further development is to occur. It is anticipated that more local people will benefit from the new employment this will generate, through emerging skill training initiatives.

STRATFORD TOWN CENTRE AND STRATFORD RAIL LANDS

LPAC has designated Stratford Town Centre within its strategic network of centres as a Major Centre with a policy thrust of regeneration (LPAC, 1996). There is considerable potential for the redevelopment of existing sites, in conjunction with the current improvements to public transport. Stratford Rail Lands provide a major development opportunity adjacent to the town centre. The Urban Framework Plan for the Rail Lands currently being drawn up by a sub-group of the Lea Valley Partnership (involving Boroughs, the Lea Valley Regional Park Authority and London & Continental Railways) is seeking to fully integrate the town centre with a mixed use development on the Rail Lands. The emphasis is on sustainable regeneration with a major business and commercial centre creating jobs for local people. LPAC regards the Rail Lands as one of the main land resources in London for large scale new site development to broaden the capital's economic base; as such it is also designated within the Strategic Employment Sites framework as an Industrial Business Park. RPG9A (DoE, 1995) indicates the Rail Lands as the focus for a wider development area including Hackney Wick, Thornton Fields and Temple Mills. Consequently it forms a key part of strategy for the Objective 2 area in East London and the Lea Valley (GOL 1995).

ROYAL DOCKS

Royal Docks are another of LPAC's Opportunity Areas and the potential for large-scale new development is recognised in 1996 Guidance (GOL 1996,A). The need to generate new employment opportunities for the established population of the area and to integrate developments with the new and proposed infrastructure improvements is emphasised. Current developments in the Western Royal Docks include the West Silvertown urban village on the south side of the Royal Victoria Dock. The first phase of this involving over 1000 new homes, a community centre, health care and retail facilities is currently under construction and parcels of land for phase 2 have been identified for a mixed development of business, leisure, retail and residential uses. A Thameside park adjacent to the Thames Barrier is also under construction. A new Royal Victoria Dock Pedestrian Bridge will link the urban village with the planned ExCel London International Exhibition Centre on the north-side of the dock. The Exhibition Centre will provide over 90,000 sqm. of conference and event space. Its realisation will be an important test for the success of the east-west strategy. In the East Royal Docks a masterplan has been drawn up for the Royals Business Park which could provide up to 140,000 sqm. of office and R&D space. Adjacent to this on the north-side of the Royal Albert Dock it is proposed to develop, by 1998, the University of East London's Docklands Campus which would include the Thames Gateway Technology Centre. The business park and hi-tech University will support LPAC's designation within the Strategic Employment Sites framework for a Technology Park in the Royal Docks. In addition the European headquarters of a healthcare company are planned for completion by 1998 on the north-side of the Albert Dock Basin.

BECKTON

Beckton is also an area of opportunity in LPAC's advice and the Governments

Guidance. It is similar to a number of locations on the north bank of the river with large scale redundant land poorly integrated into neighbouring residential areas. A number of sites remain undeveloped in the area around the A406/A13 junction. LPAC has stressed the importance of resisting further out-of-centre retail and leisure development in this area because of the impact on the vitality and viability of surrounding town centres such as Barking. However, a cinema and a hypermarket have already been built and permission has been granted subject to a planning agreement for an extension of the hypermarket and for further non-food retail development. A planning permission also exists for commercial, leisure and retail development on the former Beckton Gasworks site.

WEST HAM MILLS (THREE MILLS/ABBEY MILLS)

This former industrial area is now the focus for leisure and heritage activities in conjunction with the retention and encouragement of employment uses. Steps need to be taken to ensure that local communities in the adjacent areas benefit from potential job opportunities. Development would benefit from being in association with the enhancement of the environmental and waterside, as much of the area is within the Lea Valley Regional Park. The public transport accessibility to be gained at West Ham station should facilitate the comprehensive regeneration of this area.

EAST INDIA/LEAMOUTH

The area around Leamouth is one of London's prime industrial opportunities and as such it is part of a designated Preferred Industrial Location. It is a integral part of the ribbon of industry running north alongside the River Lea and it should be protected, enhanced and promoted. The opportunities for development which remain at East India Dock could provide associated employment uses such as light industry or R&D, integrated with existing office development.

GREENWICH WATERFRONT

Greenwich Waterfront stretches seven miles along the River Thames between Deptford and Thamesmead and has over 1000 acres of developable land. To guide change in this area the borough launched the Greenwich Waterfront Strategy in 1991 its remit is to ensure integrated physical, social and economic regeneration. The Greenwich Waterfront Development Partnership (GWDP) has been set up to act as the guardian and champion of the strategy. In addition to facilitating the development of major sites the partnership has been active in gained funding from central government, in particular under

Assisted Area status, and from Europe under the KONVER programme. The waterfront includes:-

Greenwich Peninsula/Millennium. The potential of this site for large scale employment generating development is recognised in LPAC's advice and the Government's guidance. A significant part of the peninsula is to host the Millennium Experience which is expected to create 2,000 jobs during construction and a further 5,000 jobs during operation. The site has been cleared and construction of the Millennium Dome, the centrepiece of the development, is under way. Access has been a key element in the plans. No private parking will be available on the site, except for disabled visitors. The majority of people will arrive on site by the new Jubilee Line Extension station on the peninsula, bus or coach, or by river. A concern for LPAC has been the long-term legacy of the site. The unique strategic significance it provides warrants the need for a continued world city role, integrated with residential and other uses which have previously been granted planning permission on the southern part of the peninsula.

Deptford Creek/Greenwich Reach marks the western end of the Greenwich Waterfront. The site is divided into two parts by the Creek. The smaller eastern part of the site is currently the subject of an application by Greenwich Reach 2000 Ltd to provide a cruise liner terminal, residential, leisure, hotel and retail uses. Planning permission has just been granted for the mixed-use redevelopment of the larger western part of the site. The largest land use will be residential, in conjunction with a foyer scheme for homeless and unemployed persons, commercial and retail uses and a boatyard and landing stage.

Woolwich Arsenal & Town Centre. LPAC has designated Woolwich town centre as a Major Centre with a policy thrust of regeneration (LPAC 1996). This means that there is considerable potential within the centre for new developments and the redevelopment of existing sites. The Royal Arsenal site on the riverfront, adjacent to the town centre provides a big opportunity in this respect. The former military land has been taken over by English Partnerships, whom along with the London Borough of Greenwich and the Woolwich Development Agency, have drawn up a development strategy. This seeks to open up the site, linking the town centre with the River Thames. The site has nineteen Listed Buildings and it is intended to create a conservation and heritage area around these, focusing on leisure, education, retail, business and residential.

Development will be phased to encourage use of the site as soon as possible.

An increasing transport focus

Anna Whyatt's paper in Volume 1 Number 1 drew attention to the importance of good transport in regenerating the East London economy. Comparatively poor strategic accessibility is part of the explanation for the imbalance in economic health between west and east. This has been recognised by government in the relative weight of current committed investment in new transport infrastructure, now biased in favour of the east (GOL 1996,B). GOL accepted LPAC's advice that transport improvements and promotion of new development must be taken forward in an integrated manner, with priority given to those parts of London most in need of, and offering opportunities for, regeneration. The decision to locate an international station on the Channel Tunnel Rail Link (CTRL) at Stratford, for which LPAC leant strong strategic support to the case orchestrated by Newham Council, was a success of European significance. It will be particularly important to take full advantage of this, as Heathrow's development influence on the west side of London looks set to grow.

A key element of the ELDF is the increasing transport accessibility it will enjoy. It has strengths now as a focus of existing road and rail links. These will be significantly enhanced as follows:-

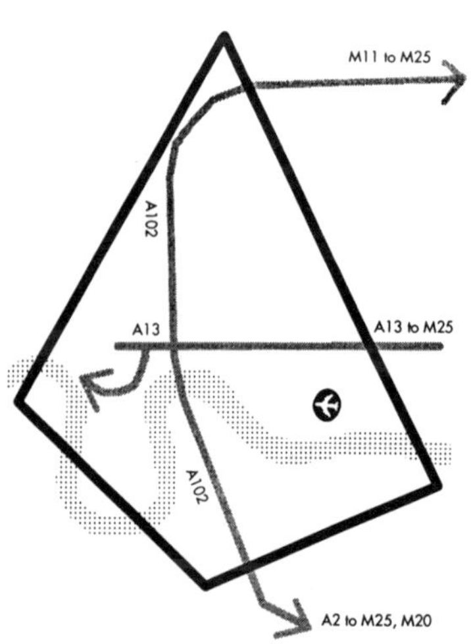

Figure 4: East London Development Focus Regional Road Links

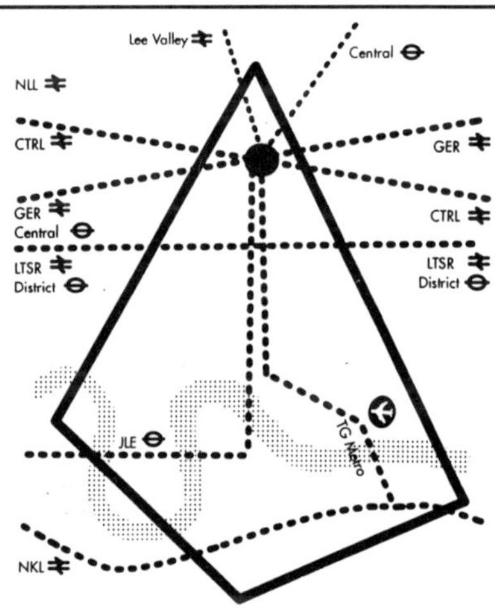

Figure 5: East London Development Focus Strategic Rail Transport Links

Roads (Figure 4): The M11 link and programmed improvements to the A13 will strengthen the ELDF's location, being where the regional links from the M25 reach Inner London at the A102. Traffic capacity towards Central London and westwards from here sharply diminishes and will increasingly be subject to restraint measures. Given effective demand management within the ELDF, particularly at Blackwall, it will benefit from comparative road transport accessibility advantage in London regional terms.

Rail (Figure 5): Stratford is already enhancing its public transport accessibility, through its new 'regional rail interchange' between the Great Eastern Railway, the North London Line and the Underground (Central Line and Jubilee Line Extension), and its associated bus station.

The Jubilee Line Extension (JLE), due to open in autumn 1998, will add considerably to the ELDF accessibility within London, with four ELDF stations in addition to its Stratford terminus. These will link the Canary Wharf business district, the Greenwich Peninsula millennium site, the interchanges at Canning Town (North London Line and Docklands Light Railway) and West Ham (District Line and the London, Tilbury & Southend Railway). London Transport has commissioned a study of the economic development impact of these and other locations on the JLE route.

The decision to include Stratford International Station in the CTRL project was based on the boost which access to the future European high speed rail network would give to regeneration in East London. These benefits will be concentrated in the ELDF, at and around Stratford and via the internal road and rail links to the Canary Wharf area, Greenwich Peninsula, the Royal Docks and the Lower Lea Valley.

River Crossings. The limited ability to cross the Thames has been one of the reasons why East London's economic recovery has lagged, dividing realisation of its economic potential. The ELDF has had to rely on the Blackwall Tunnel. The Jubilee Line Extension will provide a welcome public transport link, crossing the river three times within the area, and will be augmented by the Docklands Light Railway extension to Lewisham. GOL's Transport Strategy (GOL, 1996, B) includes three schemes for additional river crossings, all within the ELDF:-

- a rail tunnel to link the North London Line from Stratford to the North Kent Line;
- a new road bridge at Gallions Reach to link the A13 and A406 at Beckton with the A2016 'South Thames-side Development Route' at Thamesmead;

- a third road crossing at Blackwall.

GOL sees all three schemes as necessary and favours a package approach to realisation. We regard the Woolwich Rail Crossing as the priority scheme in strategic terms, particularly if conceived as part of a 'Thames Gateway Metro' concept proposed in The Woolwich Rail Tunnel (Thames Gateway Metro) Project Definition Stage Summary Report (Railtrack *et al.*, 1997). This would allow a regular quality rail service between the CTRL stations at Ebbsfleet and Stratford, via Woolwich and the Royal Docks. It would link the ELDF with the other main focus of Thames Gateway development at Kent Thames-side, and bind the two sides of the Thames together in labour market terms. It could form part of a revived east-west CrossRail project, linking the ELDF from Stratford to central and west London; this would be much more in tune with current strategic development objectives for London than the previous CrossRail's purpose of increasing capacity for Essex commuters.

Future of the East London development focus

The review of the situation at the main opportunity locations shows that considerable development activity is now occurring or in prospect. From a strategic perspective there are a number of important issues which need addressing in the immediate future, for which the ELDF can act as a co-ordination mechanism.

Of paramount importance is the need to learn lessons from the Docklands experience. Where proposals are going ahead they must result in employment opportunities for local people, particularly given the concentration of deprivation and unemployment both in and around the ELDF (Figure 1). A number of the local regeneration agencies and partnerships are promoting 'local employment initiatives' which would assist in achieving this goal. We need to find ways of working this into the planning process. Training strategies are starting to ensure that local people and communities gain fully from new developments. The successful SRB scheme for skills upgrading in the whole of Thames Gateway London should contribute towards achieving this (GOL 1996, C).

When schemes for sites are being considered, proposals for out-of-centre retail and leisure uses should be dismissed. The vulnerability of town centres within the Focus has been recognised, and they have accordingly been designated as centres in regeneration need, so further pressures on their vitality and viability must be avoided.

Where appropriate proposals could also contribute to meeting London's future housing needs, with regeneration benefits arising from the multiplier effects of residential development on the economy.

The pace of activity can quicken considerably over the next few years, particularly if the ELDF is used to provide promotional synergy. Following on from the opening of the Jubilee Line Extension next year, two events will be of especial significance:-

- The Greenwich Millennium Experience, for which construction has begun. This will draw national, European and worldwide attention to East London and provide a powerful symbol of the area's regeneration, the benefits from which need spreading over the wider area cross-river, particularly in terms of the longer-term legacy (image, employment) of the actual millennium event.
- The Channel Tunnel Rail Link with its Stratford International Station, scheduled to open in 2003. Again this is of critical symbolic significance in redressing the investment and development imbalance in favour of East London. The ELDF shows how its benefits can be maximised using the synergy between opportunities.

How East London can take maximum advantage of these two strategic catalysts now needs addressing in terms of implementation mechanisms. The LDDC will be closing its doors next Spring. The two sub-regional partnerships, Thames Gateway London and London Lea Valley, which include the local authorities and TECs, are gathering force, supported by English Partnerships, GOL and LPAC. The new Government is committed to an elected Mayor and Assembly for Greater London by 2000, supplemented by a London Development Agency. These new strategic arrangements should provide the necessary ability to reinforce the cross-London strategy and priority framework aimed at creating overall developmental balance and realising East London's potential. They can be expected to work through the sub-regional partnerships and more local mechanisms to realise the opportunities we have referred to.

We believe the ELDF should be advanced as the coordinating vehicle for the area's physical development potential, based on the synergy to be gained by conceiving these closely related opportunities and achievements as a whole. More needs doing, as plans for its component parts proceed, to establish the overall potential of the Focus, between Stratford, Canary Wharf, Greenwich and the Royals, as a new multi-site centre for East London, providing for a variety of metropolitan activities. We see these as giving the whole of East London, both sides of the river, a new vibrant heart, a source of hope and pride for East Londoners.

The authors would like to acknowledge graphics by Jenny Fender.

REFERENCES

Department of the Environment (1988) *Regional Guidance for the South East, PPG9*. London: HMSO.

Department of the Environment (1995) *The Thames Gateway Planning Framework, RPG9A*. London: HMSO.

Department of the Environment South East Regional Office (1994) *Regional Planning Guidance for the South East*, London: HMSO.

EC decisions ERDF 97.09.13.001 & ARINCO 97.UK.16.001 including *Single Programming Document for the Objective 2 area East London and the Lee Valley 1997-1999*.

GOL (1995) *Regenerating East London and the Lee Valley. A summary of the Objective 2 Single Programming Document 1994-1996*. Government Office for London.

GOL (1996, A) *Strategic Guidance for London Planning Authorities, RPG3*. London: HMSO.

GOL (1996, B) *A Transport Strategy for London*. London: HMSO

GOL (1996, C) *Single Regeneration Budget Challenge Fund Round 3. Summary of Final Bids Received*. Government Office for London.

Jones Lang Wootton (1997) Decentralisation of Offices from Central London: An Annual Special Survey - 1997. Jones Lang Wootton.

LPAC (1994) *Advice on Strategic Planning Guidance for London*. London Planning Advisory Committee.

LPAC (1996) *Supplementary Advice on Strategic Town Centres*. London Planning Advisory Committee.

Railtrack, British Rail, London Docklands Development Corporation & London Transport (1997) *Woolwich Rail Tunnel (Thames Gateway Metro) Project Definition Stage, Summary Report.*

SERPLAN (1990) *Action in the East Thames Corridor*. London: South East Regional Planning Conference.

NOTES

1. The London Planning Advisory Committee, the 33 London planning authorities' statutory joint body, to which Martin Simmons is chief planner and Abigail Warren a senior planner.

East London and the New Labour government

Stephen Timms

What will Labour's New Deal mean for East London?

East London is full of astonishing contrasts. The final item of this journal's launch issue was a review of a book about death. The author of that book, Lord Young, visited Newham recently to open an American-style funeral campus in Beckton. It stands opposite the Beckton Docklands Light Railway Station and adjoins the Asda supermarket. I have never seen anything like it before, with its manicured lawns and its brash, modern redbrick buildings. This, I suppose, is the new face of the funeral in the new East London, an undertaking business targeted at the Canary Wharf generation, light years away from the traditional East End funeral business.

And yet, and yet... These new premises are actually operated by T. Cribb & Sons, the funeral directors established in Canning Town in 1881. That is not just the local nameplate for some American funeral multinational. The present proprietor grew up in the business and is the grandson of the founder. When he retires, his sons will take over. They have had the same phone number since the telephone was invented. The Cribb name is revered in Canning Town, synonymous as it has been for generations with dignified burial. And the present prosperity of the business is due in large measure to its reintroduction in the 1980s of the traditional horse-drawn funeral cortège.

The juxtaposition of surprising continuity and rapid change is evident in many aspects of East London life. The juxtaposition which is the key to East London's future development, though, is a different one. East London has the most severe problems of urban deprivation to be found anywhere in Britain - but it also presents the most spectacular opportunities for urban regeneration in Europe.

There is a great deal at stake in the political decisions affecting East London over the next two or three decades. If we get them right, there is a once-in-a-hundred-years opportunity to change the nature of East London permanently for the better, ensuring that future generations have much better chances than previous ones, and perhaps finally ending the historic drift eastwards out of the area which started in the 1930s. If we get them wrong, the social costs could be immense and catastrophic.

No-one in East London needs to look far to find the evidence of deprivation. Ken Worpole claimed in the launch issue of *Rising East* that 'not only is the East End in a state of enormous social disrepair, but ... the worst is yet to come'. Government analysis of the 1991 census concluded that Newham is the most deprived place in the country, followed closely by Hackney and Tower Hamlets. The number of people living within five miles of Stratford who are unemployed is still not far short of 100,000. There are major problems of de-skilling, skills mismatch and the lack of specialised qualifications. At the time of the census, over 40 per cent of economically active 16-19 year olds in Hackney were unemployed.

Despite all this, East London is characterised far more by optimism than by despair. If the deprivation is obvious, it is not too hard to find the grounds for optimism - the factors which make East London Europe's most promising location for urban regeneration:

- We have enormous areas of land available for development close to central London, in the Lea Valley, the Royal Docks and along the River Thames - much of it in spectacular waterfront locations
- We have an impressive transport infrastructure which will be augmented next year by the Jubilee Line and early in the next century by the international passenger station at Stratford
- Geographically, we are the place where Europe meets London. We have a great deal to gain from increasing trade and cultural links between the UK and continental Europe
- East London is the most youthful place in the country. Newham has the highest proportion of under-fives in the country; Tower Hamlets is in second place and Hackney third. Waltham Forest is eighth and Barking and Dagenham tenth (Stationery Office 1997).

It is a fascinating and compelling place with a powerful hold on our emotions and on our imaginations. London's future is here and so are its brightest prospects. In its local authorities, its schools and colleges and its university, its regeneration partnerships, its growing churches and thriving mosques and temples, everywhere in East London there are the signs of imagination and determination being translated into actual change for the better.

To this hopeful picture we can now add one further element: the election of a Labour government on 1 May 1997. Labour's election victory unleashed a national wave of optimism which, months later, shows no sign of abating. In the following pages, I want to examine the programme the new government has announced and consider how it is likely to affect East London. I do so unashamedly as a supporter of the Government, but my contention - that the approach which is being adopted will help us greatly - is one I would be happy to defend anywhere.

The remainder of the article is divided into four main sections:

- The Government's approach: in particular, its approach to managing the economy
- The state we're in: problems in East London and how the Government's policies will address them
- The New Deal: welfare to work *will* work for East London
- The tools for regeneration: how the Government's regeneration policies will turn East London around.

The Government's approach

The Prime Minister, Tony Blair, recently characterised the Government as 'modern, fair and strong'. Central to its programme is the commitment to economic stability, to secure the higher level of investment which eluded the previous government and which East London so desperately needs. Labour's manifesto promised: *'We will provide stable economic growth with low inflation, and promote dynamic and competitive business and industry at home and abroad'.* That commitment rules out some of the approaches advocated by the Labour Party in the past. But it also holds out the prospect of sustained change for the better, enduring in the long term.

Britain's problems will not be put right overnight. We can, however, point the economy in a different direction, start to decrease the inequality in our communities and then - not in one term of government but over the course of two, three or four - steadily make the changes we all want to see.

It is important to reflect first on what we believe to be right. At the heart of progressive politics there remains a belief in equality. Over the last two decades, Britain has become increasingly unequal, and East London has suffered the cold blast of these economic changes with particular acuteness.

The commitment to equality

Those of us who prize equality as our goal have often been forced to explain, defensively, what we do *not* mean by it. We do not mean that everyone is born with equal talents - we know that is not true. We do not mean that we expect everyone to earn the same amount. So what do we mean?

Richard Crossman called it 'fair shares'. That meant, he said, 'feeling as a community that things are fairly distributed ... that people are feeling, roughly speaking, that they are getting what they deserve' (Crossman 1951). R. H. Tawney saw equality as not 'an identical level of pecuniary incomes' but as 'equality of environment, of access to education and the means of civilisation, of security and independence, and of the social consideration which equality in these matters usually carries with it...' (Tawney, 1931).

This tone is echoed in new Labour's approach. Gordon Brown said before the election in the Crosland Memorial Lecture:

> What has happened over the last two decades - the Tory exaltation of inequality - has made it all the more necessary to make the philosophical case for equality ... I believe that everyone should have the chance to bridge the gap between what they are and what they have it in themselves to become ... our commitment to equality is as strong as ever.[1]

That is the commitment at the heart of Labour's economic strategy - and in East London, it has a deep resonance with our experiences over the past twenty years. Some may be surprised at the ambition of Gordon Brown's economic programme. They should not be.

The Government faces a huge task. It is very striking that, consistently, after the war, income inequality decreased, until 1979. Almost the day after the election in 1979 the trend reversed and inequality started to grow again. What has happened since 1979 is crystal clear and unambiguous. The gap has expanded into a chasm.

The Institute for Fiscal Studies (IFC) found in 1994 that the gap between the highest wages and the lowest in the UK was the biggest since records began. The top 20 per cent of earners take 67 per cent of total income. The proportion taken by the bottom 20 per cent has fallen from 14 per cent to 9 per cent since 1979. The bottom tenth take just 2½ per cent of total income (Goodman and Webb 1994). A recent IFS study argues that this inequality is intensifying - and it also shows that London is by far the most unequal part of the country (Goodman, Johnson and Webb 1997).

Last year in a survey, 90 per cent - including a majority even of the highest earners - said the gap between the highest and lowest incomes is now excessive (Stationery Office 1996). People's moral sense tells them this inequality is wrong, but it defies the laws of economic sense as well. Inequality does not work. Will Hutton has shown how, in the upturn from 1981 to 1988, and the recession that followed, everybody suffered because of the growing inequality in Britain (Hutton 1995). The whole economy was dragged down, not just the poor.

Yawning inequality hurts everyone. Through our taxes, we all pay for unemployment. In 1979, we spent twice as much on education as on the costs of unemployment. Today we spend more on unemployment than on the whole of education. No wonder our schools are hard up.

Once we embark on this downward slope, it is very difficult to stop. Crime flourishes as jobs disappear and people look elsewhere for a living. It was Michael Heseltine who said, twelve years ago: 'Against a background of high unemployment, the invitation to crime becomes more appealing. Idleness becomes a resentment that gives crime an indefensible normality (Heseltine 1985).' How right he was.

The twin arguments against inequality, moral and economic, were summed up by the former US Labor Secretary, Robert Reich, writing in the *Financial Times* just before the election. The article was called 'The menace to prosperity' and sub-headed 'Widening inequality poses a growing threat to US and other societies'. It described the very different economic experiences of the badly off and the well off in recent years. 'There is no escaping the underlying moral question,' Reich said, 'which is also a political one ... are we or are we not still in this together?'[2]

If Labour's economic programme is shorn of some of the rhetoric of the past, its ambition is as great as ever and its effectiveness will be greater. There will be partnership rather than confrontation, pragmatism and imagination rather than dogma. The goal is an inclusive society in which the gulf between rich and poor narrows rather than just getting wider - and East London stands to gain immense benefit from that change.

The state we're in

In East London we stand to benefit from this change in direction more than anyone, because those who have been or are on the brink of being excluded make up such a large proportion of our communities. The statistics are depressing - but they are a baseline assessment by which we can measure our achievement in the years ahead.

The three boroughs that constitute the narrowest definition of East London[3] maintain an unhappy grip on the highest positions in the Government's deprivation index, based on the 1991 census. Newham is ranked top of all English local authority areas for its *degree* of deprivation. Tower Hamlets is top of the list for *intensity* of deprivation and Hackney has the highest *extent* of deprivation. All three boroughs are among the top ten in each of the three measures.[4] They alone contain twenty-two of Greater London's fifty most deprived wards (Edwards and Flatley 1996). Some of this deprivation has rippled outwards into Waltham Forest and Barking and Dagenham. This broad measure, summarising a wide number of indicators, shows in essence that East London is the neediest part of the country.

Other indicators of need tell the same story. Hackney and Tower Hamlets are the only boroughs in London where more than six out of ten households do not have a car. The same two boroughs have the highest number of children living in households where no-one earns a wage. Newham is also well above average on both these measures (Edwards and Flatley 1996).

UNEMPLOYMENT AND LOW PAY

Unemployment is higher in East London, at 20.1 per cent, than anywhere else in Greater London, where the average is 10.8 per cent. Among East London men, unemployment is 26.3 per cent, and where figures are available for particularly vulnerable groups, they are much worse. Self-reported unemployment among ethnic minority men in Tower Hamlets, for example, runs at over 40 per cent.

Two groups will be the beneficiaries in East London of the Government's flagship 'New Deal' to tackle unemployment: the nine thousand people over 25 who have been unemployed for more than two years, and over five thousand under 25s have been out of work for six months or more. The 'New Deal' is the cornerstone of the programme to tackle disadvantage and is described in detail in the next section.

For many of those in work, wages remain low by London standards. The statutory minimum wage which the Government will introduce will help. Raising the minimum wage will also increase the incentive to work - wage levels in some sectors are currently so low that people cannot afford to come off benefit to take on jobs there.

HOUSING

Homelessness in East London might seem to have been always with us, but when I entered local politics in Newham in 1984, there were thirty homeless families in the whole of the borough. The homelessness working party to which I was appointed, determined that it wanted every one of the families to be in a permanent home in time for Christmas - and achieved that goal.

Last year, over 1500 families were accepted as homeless in Newham, Hackney and Tower Hamlets. That amounted to ten in every thousand households in Newham and Tower Hamlets, and thirteen in every thousand in Hackney. In England, the average is less than six in every thousand.[5] The last Housing Act tackled the problem simply by reducing the help available to homeless families, reviving the spectre of families being moved every couple of years from one insecure home to the next, and of children being brought up not knowing what it is to have a secure home. That was no answer, and I am delighted that the Government has moved quickly to restore local authorities' duties to homeless people.

Overcrowding is also more common in East London, particularly in Tower Hamlets, where 11 per cent of households have more than one person per room. The Greater London average is just over 4 per cent (Edwards and Flatley 1996). The condition of the housing stock is poor. Later in this article I shall look at the Government's provision of additional resources for housing investment.

THE HEALTH SERVICE

Our health service is stretched almost to the point of breaking. The Conservative government's funding formula for the NHS treated areas like East London appallingly. The extra funds found for health in Labour's first Budget have eased the worst fears about the survival of clinical services through the coming winter, but East London will continue to be hit disproportionately hard until we replace the present funding formula with a fairer one.

The previous government's formula was based on work carried out by health economists at York University, but then adjusted by officials at the Department of Health who decided that there should be no needs weighting for that part of the formula relating to community health services, about a quarter of the total. In 1995, an article in *Health Service Journal* presented the top ten losers from this adjustment. East London suffered the largest cash loss to its target - £13.2 million. The other biggest losers were Manchester, Liverpool, Sunderland, Barnsley, North Durham, St Helen's and Knowsley, South of Tyne, Tees and Newcastle (Hacking 1995).

The Secretary of State for Health at the time was Virginia Bottomley, the MP for south-west Surrey. The biggest gainer of all from the adjustment, with more than a 5 per cent increase, was mid-Surrey. The second biggest gainer in the entire country was north-west Surrey. The third biggest was south-west Surrey, and the fourth was east Surrey. With this sort of 'pork-barrel' politics to contend with, it is not surprising that our health service has had such a struggle.

When Stephen Dorrell was Health Secretary, the resource allocation formula was improved, but it continues to undercount populations in highly mobile areas, it fails to account for extra costs associated with specific communities and it is yet to be comprehensively weighted for need.

Under the Tory changes, every health authority and trust board member was appointed directly by the Secretary of State. Nobody wanted to rock the boat by pointing out what was happening. Frank Dobson has taken the first steps in opening up the appointment process, but the new government also needs to reintroduce the sense of accountability to the communities being served which the Tories effectively destroyed.

EDUCATION

In education, the strenuous efforts of East London's authorities in recent years are proving slow to bear fruit. Table 1 shows the ranking of Newham, Tower Hamlets and Hackney on a range of indicators. Most worrying is the poor performance of children in English, Maths and Science at the end of primary school, where the three boroughs have a near-total grip of the bottom three places on the list. GCSE performance is slightly better (particularly in Newham, as a result of a great deal of consistent hard work over a decade). Pupil absence is high in primary schools.

Nearly 6,500 five, six and seven year olds in the six East London

Table 1: Relative educational achievement of East London boroughs (out of 32 Greater London boroughs)

	Hackney	Newham	Tower Hamlets
Primary English	30	31	32
Primary Maths	31	32	30
Primary Science	32	31	29
5 GCSEs (A*-C)	28	26	31
5 GCSEs (A*-G)	28	20	29
1 GCSE (A*-G)	17	16	22
NVQ achievement	26	18	25

NOTES

"Primary English/Maths/Science": The percentage of eligible pupils achieving the level expected of most 11 year olds in the relevant subject as shown by the standard test at Key Stage 2

"5 GCSEs A*-C": The percentage of 15 year olds who gained five or more GCSEs at grades A*-C

"5 GCSEs A*-G": The percentage of 15 year olds who gained five or more GCSEs at grades A*-G

"1 GCSE+A*-G": The percentage of 15 year olds who gained one or more GCSEs at grades A*-G

"NVQ achievement": The percentage achieving all the vocational qualifications or units for which they studied in 1995/96

Source: DfEE performance tables, 1997

boroughs are currently taught in classes of more than thirty pupils.[6] All of those children will have smaller class sizes under the Government's proposals, with funding made available by abolishing the assisted places scheme. The strong commitment to raising standards in schools expressed in July's Education White Paper - including the establishment of education action zones where special help is needed - gives us the chance for substantial progress in East London.

CRIME

Crime is too high in East London. Nearly 86,000 offences were notified to police in the three boroughs in 1993/94 - an increase of a third on 1981 (Edwards and Flatley 1996). Notifiable offences, of course, are only the tip of the iceberg. House of Commons figures which uprate recorded offences to account for apparent under-reporting suggest that in the year ending June 1995, there was one burglary for every ten households in Tower Hamlets (the same as the Greater London average), one for every nine households in Newham and one for every five in Hackney.

This is not a record to be proud of, but East London does not stand out as badly on crime statistics as it does on the other indicators reviewed so far. Is it fanciful to believe that the survival of communities in East London, and the strength of the newer ethnic minority communities which dominate much of the new East London, provide some degree of protection against crime?

Jack Straw has announced a major review of the criminal justice system. Early specific proposals include speeding up the system for dealing with young offenders and introducing a new offence of racial harassment which will be particularly valuable in East London.

In setting out these facts I do not suggest they are permanent. Trends are there to be broken. There have been many changes for the better achieved by local authorities, City Challenge partnerships, London Docklands Development Corporation and others. But we need to recognise where we are, so we can take the first steps forward to where we want to be. Our destination is certainly some way off, but our vision is very bright.

The New Deal

Labour said before the election that the top priority was to attack the waste of unemployment among young people. That waste is one of the last government's most destructive legacies. Allowing young people to slip into the spiral of unemployment leading to unemployability, alternating between low-wage and no-wage, spending less and less on educating and training them for work and more and more on the welfare payments that are the bills of government failure - this is the legacy we inherited on May 1st.

The challenge that faces us is immense, but the mandate we received at the election for our programme of change was unprecedented, and the new Government is determined to deliver. In June 1997, the Prime Minister set out his analysis of the poverty and worklessness which Britain faces. He said:

> We need to act in a new way because fatalism and not just poverty is the problem we face ... the crushing belief that things cannot get any better. I want to give people back the will to win again. This will to win is what drives a country, the belief that expectations can be fulfilled and ambitions realised (Blair 1997).

I think we have that will to win in East London. There is a huge enthusiasm for the future, the beginnings of a culture that fosters publications like this one, a willingness to embrace change and to see the opportunities that lie ahead. If we are really to succeed, though, we need a huge effort to rid our communities of the misery of youth unemployment.

When a significant proportion of our young people enter the job market and find themselves ill-equipped for the opportunities that are available, they begin the descent towards unemployability. East London is more affected by the unemployment of young people than almost anywhere in the country. That is why I was delighted that the eradication of youth and long-term unemployment was a central feature of our election campaign - and it remains the Government's central objective now we are in office.

The New Deal will be funded over the life of the present Parliament by over £3 billion from the windfall tax being levied on the privatised utilities. It will be a serious programme, driven by passionate commitment at the heart of government, characterised by high quality and providing real opportunities to help young people and others into work.

HOW IT WILL WORK

The programme will target two groups:

- young people aged 18 to 24 who have been unemployed for more than six months
- older people who have been unemployed for more than two years.

A disproportionately large number in these target groups live in East London. Over 1% of those in the first group nationwide live in Newham, another 1%

in Tower Hamlets and well over 1% in Hackney.[7]

The first group will be offered choices from four options:

- work with a private sector employer, with the employer being offered £60 per week for six months as a contribution to the costs of taking on the young person
- work with the new Environment Taskforce; participants will continue to receive their benefit plus a premium equivalent to about £15 per week
- work on similar terms with a voluntary sector organisation
- full time education or training for up to 12 months, either in basic skills or leading to a relevant vocational qualification, without loss of benefit.

Older, long term unemployed people will have access to two of the options:

- work with a private sector employer, in this case with the employer receiving £75 per week for six months
- full-time education or training.

Pilots of the New Deal for young people will begin in January 1998; the full national programme will begin in April. The initiative for the long-term unemployed will start in June.

Each person taking part in the New Deal will enter through a 'Gateway' - an intensive period of counselling and guidance. With this help, many young people will find work straightaway. Others will need help to improve their basic skills before progressing to one of the four New Deal options. They will be provided with it. Every option will include at least one day each week of training leading to accredited qualifications. Every participant in the New Deal will have an employment service caseworker assigned to help them before, during and after their participation in the programme.

The New Deal also extends to lone parents. Those with children of school age are already being invited to Job Centres for advice on opportunities. To help this group, the childcare costs disregard in benefits is being raised from £60 to £100 per week for families with two or more children. There will also be special help within the New Deal for people with disabilities.

THE NEW DEAL MAKES SENSE

The New Deal will help 250,000 young people during the course of this Parliament, and tens of thousands of long term unemployed people. Without work, people cannot take control of their lives. They cannot be responsible for themselves, and they cannot therefore be responsible for what happens around them. Work is the foundation of everything else. It fosters pride and self-respect; responsibility; and a sense of community.

The New Deal will also contribute to the regeneration of local communities, not just through the move from welfare into work, and the provision of training, but directly, through environmental and voluntary work carried out by the young people on the New Deal. The resources being committed to the New Deal are sufficient to ensure that the work being carried out meets an actual need, not activity artificially created and to no real purpose. You cannot restore people's self-confidence and self-respect by asking them to carry out pointless tasks. There is plenty of real work to be tackled, but it takes commitment and imagination to bring together the work to be done and the people to do it. That is what the New Deal will do.

THE IMPORTANCE OF QUALITY AND CHOICE

The New Deal is not another Government scheme. If it is going to work, it will need to be claimed and owned by all sections of society. The business sector, the voluntary sector, local government and the trade unions will all need to play their part. This has to be a national crusade to tackle unemployment, and the indications so far are encouraging that it will attract strong support from all the key players.

There is a further reason why quality is paramount. The Government has been clear about the duties which the New Deal will place upon young people. Their duty, in return for a choice of New Deal places, is to participate fully in being trained and finding work. This is fair enough, as long as what is being offered is a quality package. An indefinite stay on full benefit will not be an option.

This position is the right one. It is based on a balance of rights and duties. It recognises the responsibility of the Government, and the responsibility of the individual. That is the 'Deal' part of the New Deal. The Government, with its partners, offers quality opportunities; the young person plays his or her part. Quality is the linchpin on which this arrangement rests.

THE ROLE OF PARTNERSHIPS

I want the people of East London to 'claim' the New Deal as their own. The key, as in many other areas of the new government's activity, is partnership.

We are used to partnership in East London. The campaign for the international passenger station on the Channel Tunnel Rail Link at Stratford, for example, was a successful public - private sector initiative, bringing together all those who will benefit from the development, including the local community. There have been other, spectacularly successful regeneration partnerships in East London, and it came as no surprise that Newham was the first borough to host its own launch of the New Deal. The Government will make use of existing partnerships where that is appropriate, build on existing arrangements, and encourage partnership of an extent, a closeness and an innovation rarely seen in the past.

There will be no national model imposed by Whitehall. The New Deal will support local proposals, made by local authorities, training and enterprise councils, voluntary sector organisations and partnerships, because the Government believes that is the way to promote initiatives which will work in each area. Each area is different and will require a different approach, and the Government will depend on proposals being developed by partnerships formed locally.

We need to ensure that people where the New Deal is operating, both employed and unemployed, feel that there is something in it for them. In addition, I hope the New Deal will help foster that sense of society, of mutual interest and responsibility, that is so lacking at the moment. I hope it will build bridges between the young people who participate in it and the communities in which it operates. The environmental task force and the voluntary sector options will be particularly important in involving the local communities. I hope they will provide a link between young unemployed people and the other members of the community which will encourage greater understanding and communication between them.

WHERE WILL THE PERMANENT JOBS COME FROM?

It is sometimes pointed out - rightly - that the New Deal will fail if there are no permanent jobs for participants to move in to at the end. That is why the Government is determined to create the conditions of economic stability in which investment and the creation of new jobs can flourish. The challenge in East London is not only to attract jobs - the jobs are coming - but to equip people who live in East London for those jobs. That is why the New Deal is so important for us.

But it is also true that the New Deal, by raising the skill levels in the workforce, can itself help to create new jobs. There are in some areas, such as information technology, serious skill shortages today. The New Deal can contribute to relieving them. For example, one computer maintenance company plans to re-train its existing experienced engineers for more highly skilled work which it does not currently have the capacity to take on. It will use the New Deal to help it recruit currently unemployed people to take over the basic maintenance work. The International Monetary Fund, in its annual report on the British economy, specifically welcomed the New Deal for this potential to 'develop human potential' and enhance employability.

There are growing signs that the creative industries can provide substantial new employment in East London, building on the wealth of our cultural diversity and the growing self-confidence of the black British communities. The 'London Bridge' soap opera is made at the thriving new film studios at Three Mills Island; East Londoners are flocking to Newham Community College's music and multimedia technology courses; and Hackney claims the biggest community of artists in the country. The growing importance of these industries has been recognised by the Prime Minister, who wrote in the *Guardian*[8] of the onset of a second industrial revolution - 'defined in part by new information technology, but also by creativity'. He pointed out that more people now work in film and television than in the car industry. With our facilities and the talents of our people, East London can be at the forefront of the creative revolution.

Tools for regeneration

While the New Deal provides the basis for a specific and concrete opportunity to rekindle the economy in East London, the Government has also proposed a very much wider range of new initiatives which will extend the push for regeneration here.

During the past ten years East London has been subject to many attempts at regeneration, the majority of which have been honestly and enthusiastically embraced by our communities and our organisational base, including local government. There have been very impressive achievements too, in London Docklands, with the City Challenge programmes in Stratford, Bethnal Green and Dalston and by the more recent programmes supported by the single regeneration budget. However, when I was Leader of Newham Council, there was obvious wasteful fragmentation, with many new agencies created to manage specific new programmes: Urban Development Corporations, HATs, TECs, Task Forces, City Challenges, EU Monitoring Committees, Sub-Regional Groups and Regeneration Partnerships.

There have been high costs due to the levels of multiplicity and fragmentation that such 'multi-agency' approaches bring about. These costs include the difficulties in co-ordinating the various agencies to work together, the lack of a single framework for evaluation and impact measurement, and often the absence of local accountability through elected leadership.

LONDON GOVERNMENT

In this context, the major theme of the Labour government's plans for London is the restoration of accountability to local people through a Mayor for London and the creation of an efficient Greater London Authority (GLA). Initial proposals suggest that the 'slimline' GLA will have oversight over regeneration and planning, and will provide a mechanism for a co-ordinated approach and a more strategic deployment of resources across London.

This has to be good news for East London, firstly because the 'beauty parade' type competitions for public regeneration cash have been very wasteful and ad hoc in their distribution of funds, and secondly because wider decisions about the locations of other major initiatives (exhibition centres, international rail stations, new stadia and so on) need to be part of a city-wide plan for regeneration, overseen by a single entity.

A recent Fabian pamphlet by my colleague Margaret Hodge, MP for Barking, spelled out the benefits that the mayor should bring. The mayor will be leader of London's continuing renaissance and will provide the political will to ensure that a balance between all London's areas is achieved. The mayor will understand that the whole of London's health depends on the regeneration of its poorest areas and the maximisation of the opportunities created by the cycles of economic change. In East London, our industrial restructuring has hit the local population very hard in terms of unemployment, and left large tracts of land still in need of adaptive re-use; London's new mayor will understand the urgency to renew East London's economy rather than over-heating the city centre and the west.

REGIONAL DEVELOPMENT

Alongside the mayor and GLA there will be a London Development Agency, and other agencies for each of the other regions of England. These initiatives are particularly welcome to those working in regeneration because they provide some of the tools required to ensure that the job gets done.

The Deputy Prime Minister, John Prescott, has long been a friend of East London. As Shadow Transport Secretary in the late 1980s, he was an early champion of the international passenger station at Stratford. When he created the new 'superministry' of Environment, Transport and the Regions, he had the interest of areas like ours at heart. Anyone who has been involved in the efforts to regenerate East London over the past few years will know that the linkage of regeneration initiatives with environmental enhancement is essential in places like Stratford, Spitalfields, Leyton and Dalston. Many will also have realised that transport infrastructure and the siting of new improved transport hubs is a critical engine of regeneration, and that a regional approach is required to ensure even development across a dense metropolitan area like London. The new Department provides the right combination of authorities to make sure such linkages are made. The

Development Agency that Dick Caborn is now consulting on will provide a single mechanism to make those links through the involvement of public, private and community representatives.

Both John Prescott and Dick Caborn have made it clear that they see the better usage of existing resources and assets as critical to achieving more from the Government's regeneration spending. This theme is reflected in many of their other new proposals, and I think they are right to try to 'sweat' our resources and assets further.

Foremost among these proposals are Dick Caborn's plans to revise the use of the Single Regeneration Budget (SRB) to focus more closely on a 'needs-led' approach, targeting the cash towards partnerships and programmes which can add real value to the lives of the hardest-pressed communities and people. For East London, this does not guarantee us additional funds. Rather it presents us with a challenge to make sure we bring forward proposals that can fully utilise the resources available - and an acknowledgement that the very tough statistics I have already described in relation to East London will secure for us our fair share of help. Regeneration proposals will be expected also to reflect the priorities in the 'New Deal'.

BOOSTING INVESTMENT IN REGENERATION

In addition to this welcome change to the SRB, Local Government Minister Hilary Armstrong has announced proposals for innovative regeneration pilot projects involving local government in partnership with others to help show new ways of achieving regeneration. Given the excellent plans already being worked up by the Thames Gateway London and Lea Valley / East London Partnerships, and the experiments being made with local investment of pension funds by East London boroughs, I hope that strong proposals will reach Hilary from our area in the first round.

At the Treasury, ministers are overseeing a comprehensive review of spending and have revamped and relaunched the Private Finance Initiative (PFI). As part of the review, initiatives of the last government such as Business Links and TECs are being carefully considered to see if there are ways, within the Development Agency structure, to enable them to provide a better service. Under the new PFI, it will be possible to finance a wide range of initiatives including hospitals, schools and major leisure facilities. Making this work in East London will require boldness and imagination from public sector institutions.

A new structure for London Transport, allowing private finance to be applied to the disgraceful condition of London Underground, will be a critical test case for the effectiveness of the new approach to public private partnerships.

There is a strong link here with Hilary Armstrong's arrangements for the phased release of capital receipts from the sale of local authority housing. Money accumulated from council house sales will be released to fund new house-building and the improvement of old stock, over a five year period. In East London, one of the key areas of regeneration need is in housing, and there is scope for imaginative links between community-based initiatives on housing estates and wider economic development programmes. This additional resource will ensure that a bottom-up dimension to regeneration continues in East London throughout this Parliament.

The Budget allocated an initial release of £784 million in capital receipts in England over the next two years. How this is to be divided between different local authorities will be decided shortly, after consultation with interested groups. However, using the proposals that the Government put out for consultation as an illustrative guide, table 2 shows how East London boroughs could benefit. On the Government's illustrative proposal, where allocations are weighted first according to local housing need and second according to the level of receipts held by the local authority, East London's six boroughs would benefit from a £50 million injection in the next two years - more than six per cent of the English total.

Table 2: Illustration of possible distribution to East London boroughs of initial release of capital receipts, based on the Government's consultation paper

Resources distributed on the following basis:

Figures shown in £m	100% in proportion to cumulative housing receipts set-aside 1990/91 to 1995/96	100% in proportion to housing need, measured by 1997/98 GNI allocations	2/3 in proportion to GNI scores, 1/3 in proportion to cumulative housing set-aside
Barking & Dagenham	4.8	6.5	5.9
Hackney	7.9	17.5	14.3
Newham	5.8	12.0	9.9
Redbridge	4.5	3.5	3.9
Tower Hamlets	8.1	12.8	11.2
Waltham Forest	3.5	6.7	5.6
Total East London	34.6	59.6	50.4

Source: 'Consultation Paper setting out proposals for implementing the Government's Capital Receipts Initiative', Department of the Environment, Transport & the Regions, June 1997.

Additional proposals concern:

- the preference for a transfer of public assets out of public control where better value can be achieved, which can be a very effective means to empower local communities as well as a mechanism for creating new wealth. Community organisations who have assets transferred to them can become less dependent on grant regimes and more able to direct their own futures.
- a reworking of the Uniform Business Rate, so that at least a portion is available for flexible spending in consultation with businesses, to help create a local 'contract' between the partners to support regeneration
- greater flexibility for local authorities in regeneration and economic development, easing some of the restrictions in the 1989 Local Government and Housing Act which have prevented local authorities from engaging in much entrepreneurial activity - activity which could support regeneration.

THE NATIONAL LOTTERY

There will also continue to be financial assistance available from the lottery and millennium funds, redirected by Chris Smith's desire to see these going in greater proportions to locally-based initiatives. These will offer opportunities for local activity in East London in the arts and culture, as well as more traditional regeneration initiatives. The Millennium Experience itself, housed in the Greenwich Dome, will provide a new spur to development and regeneration in East London which we must take care not to squander.

THE EUROPEAN UNION

East London has benefited substantially from European Union support over the past three years following the revision of the map for assisted areas in 1993. With our Objective 2 (industrial regeneration) status set to continue, new EU Urban and Defence related funding coming on-stream, and other funds for small firms about to be introduced, EU investment in East London will continue to play an important additional role. Moreover, the new Labour government is committed to maximising the benefit of EU allocations, taking up the funds fully, and is keen to see elected local leaders playing a role in decisions on the disbursement of the funds.

NEW THINKING

In addition, the election of the new government has sparked off a wide range of new and creative thinking about how regeneration should be carried forward in the next era. This has resulted in discussions about how Social Enterprise Zones, where the rules are changed at the local level to make the benefits and social support systems work more flexibly for local people, might be piloted in East London. Entrepreneurial voluntary sector projects like Community Links in Canning Town and the Bromley-by-Bow Centre are making important contributions to this new thinking.

Equally, the notion of a Town Improvement Zone (TIZ) where the businesses and other organisations clustered around large and small town centres might collaborate on financing and managing additional services to make the area work better for business, is being considered. Based loosely on the US model of the Business Improvement District, the TIZ could equally be appropriate for Ilford, Barking, Walthamstow, Green Street, London Fields, Mile End and Leytonstone.

All of us concerned about the regeneration of East London can look forward to a very much bigger tool box as a result of the new government's plans.

Conclusion

East London is an exciting place. It has energy and diversity. It has huge problems, but it also has the determination to tackle them. With the new government, it will have a powerful ally as it does so. The new programmes already announced have a clear focus on the problems which East London needs to address, and on supporting local initiatives to tackle them.

The cynical view that a Labour government would not make any difference was dispelled within a couple of days of the election. Now, it is up to us to make the most of the opportunities which the new Government will offer to us. This is a once-in-a-generation chance - and I am optimistic that East London will exploit it to the full.

I am grateful to Greg Clark of Greater London Enterprise for his help with section 5.

REFERENCES

Blair, A., The Will to Win,

British Social Attitudes Survey, (1996) London: HMSO.

Crossman, R.H.S., (1951) *Socialist Values in a Changing Civilisation*, London: The Fabian Society.

Edwards, P. and J. Flatley (eds), (1996) *The Capital Divided*, London: London Research Centre.

Goodman, A. and S. Webb, *The Distribution of UK Household Expenditure*, Institute of Fiscal Studies, London 1994.

Goodman, A., P. Johnson and S. Webb, (1997) *Inequality in the UK*, Oxford: Oxford University Press.

Hacking, J., 'For Richer, for Poorer'. *Health Service Journal*: 22.

Heseltine, M. *Where There's a Will............................1985.*

Hutton, W., (1995) *The State We're In*, London : Jonathan Cape.

Regional Trends, (1997) London : HMSO.

Tawney, R.H., (1931) *Equality*, London: Allen and Unwin.

NOTES

1. *The Anthony Crosland Memorial Lecture*, 13 February 1997.

2. *The Financial Times*, 3 March 1997.

3. The London Boroughs of Newham, Hackney and Tower Hamlets. Statistics on 'East London' refer to these three, unless indicated otherwise. The phrase 'the six East London boroughs' refers to these three plus Barking and Dagenham, Redbridge and Waltham Forest. The article also refers in a number of places to Havering.

4. *Hansard*, 7 July 1997.

5. *Hansard*, 10 July 1997.

6. *Ibid*.

7. *Hansard*, 8 July 1997.

8. *The Guardian*, 22 July 1997.

TRENDS EAST

Business concerns and attitudes in London East:

An analysis of the pan-London Employer Survey 1996

David Dundon Smith

The current trend report presents the results of the pan-London Employers Survey 1996 for the London East subregion. The pan-London Employers Survey aims to collect baseline information on business performance and attitudes across Greater London as a whole, and has been carried out annually since 1992. Data for the London East subregion however only became available last year. This trend report will therefore be the first in a series of reports on the pan-London Employer Survey. Where appropriate, the current report will draw comparisons with the London East Training and Enterprise Council (LETEC) area and London as a whole, and analyse the survey results in relation to official statistics; namely, Census of Employment[1] *and VAT registration data.*

Introduction

The London economy continues to be characterised by uneven patterns of development and business performance that undermines the revitalisation of local economies and sustainable employment in the capital. There is a sharp contrast in the fortunes of the vibrant central business district of the City and West End, and the prevalence of decay and deprivation in inner city districts. Through the latter half of this century there has been a shift in the relative fortunes of East and West London. While dock-related employment and manufacturing industry in general experienced decline in the former, inward investment and improved transport, both motorway and airport, communications expanded the importance of the latter.

The Thames Gateway London initiative seeks to re-establish the strategic importance of London East, promoting the subregion as London's corridor to continental Europe. Local authorities and agencies, through a comprehensive programme of physical investment, business support and the training of local people in the skills for the future, are working together to redress the economic imbalance across the capital and create the necessary linkages in development along the Thames Gateway corridor to sustain competitiveness into the next century.

As markets grow and entry becomes easier, businesses come under increasing pressure to assess their current practices in light of existing and potential competitors. Local economies need to benchmark levels of performance against the wider area. The London East sub-region, including the key business districts of the Docklands, City Fringe and Stratford, with its traditional strengths in manufacturing and distribution, has the potential to rival the prosperity generally experienced to the west of London.

The pan-London Employer Survey

Since 1992, the eight[2] London Training and Enterprise Councils (TECs) have collaborated in a common survey of employer organisations in the region. The survey is the most comprehensive survey of its kind in London and provides a rich source of data to map business performance and competitiveness. Survey findings have been published in London-wide reports

Map 1. Map of London / London East area

(London TECs 1997) and internal reports for participating TEC areas.

The survey aims to highlight the characteristics, needs and attitudes among businesses in London to inform the development of training and business support services and programmes managed by the TECs and their partners. A second objective of the survey has been to identify a series of indicators in business structures, corporate strategies and human resource development that can measure the competitiveness of establishments in London. The data produced can therefore provide a common benchmark of performance for sub-regional and local employers against the London-wide picture.

This report is an analysis of the 1996 survey data for the London East (Thames Gateway London) subregion and provides a baseline picture of employer organisations from which to measure the impact of regeneration programmes in the area. In this analysis, the data covers only the ten London boroughs of the London East sub-region - Barking & Dagenham, Bexley, Greenwich, Hackney, Havering, Lewisham, Newham, Redbridge, Tower Hamlets and Waltham Forest - which excludes the London Borough of Southwark and the estuary districts of Thurrock and Dartford (see Map 1). Six of these boroughs make up the LETEC area; namely, Barking & Dagenham, Havering, Newham, Redbridge, Tower Hamlets and Waltham Forest. It has been possible to include LETEC and London-wide figures from the 1994 survey in many cases to allow longitudinal comparisons to be made.

The 1996 survey was based on telephone interviews with 3,800 senior managers across London; the sample for the London East area was 780 establishments. The survey samples were stratified by size of establishment (number of employees) and industrial sector. Medium (25-199 employees) and large (200 or more employees) establishments were over-sampled to produce sufficient numbers for analysis, with the final data weighted to be representative of all establishments. Where percentages in tables and charts do not add up to a 100 per cent this may be accounted for by 'don't know' or 'not stating' responses.

The first section of this report will set out the structure and dynamics of the London East business base, including a look at the decision-making status and functional specialism of establishments. This report then examines corporate linkages and strategies, in terms of the customer- and supplier-base of local businesses. Finally, human resource issues are discussed, focusing on skill shortages, recruitment and training.

Structure and dynamics of London East business

Structure of the business base

The scale and importance of London's business sector in relation to the national and international economy cannot be underestimated. It contributes 175 of national output and is home to over 500 corporate headquarters, including half of the country's leading companies. London's importance is characterised however by the role business establishments play in wider corporate networks, whether they are headquarters or branches, and whether they perform primarily operational or service-support type functions. A recent study (London TECs, 1996) has identified the functional strengths that dominate in London – decision-making, logistics and innovation – and which interconnect in sustaining the capital's competitiveness.

Viewing London's businesses in terms of their decision-making power and the actual activities undertaken at establishments can give a better understanding of the management and human resource issues affecting employers. The pan-London Employer Survey has drawn on the above analysis to extend the definition of business structures beyond industrial sectors to encompass other characteristics. This section of the report, after a look at official statistics, analyses survey data for the London East sub-region on the decision-making status and functional activity of establishments. It then goes on to look at the dynamics in the business base according to a number of indicators.

According to the Annual Employment Survey in 1995, there were approximately 38,000 establishments in the 10 London East boroughs. This represents a fall of nearly 2,000 establishments since 1991, or 5 per cent. A similar decline in the size of the business base was evident for the LETEC area (5.5 per cent), while the number of establishments across London as a whole fell only marginally (1.6 per cent) between 1991 and 1995 (providing further evidence of the contrasting fortunes of east and west London). More significantly, whereas the business base across London dipped sharply in the early 1990s recession and bounced back with 4.5 per cent growth between 1993 and 1995, the London East business base continued to decline.

Such headline figures disguise, however, considerable variation between industrial sectors and longer-term structural changes in the sub-regional business base (see Figure 1). Distribution, including retail, hotels and restaurants, and finance and business services have both experienced growth in the number of establishments between 1991 and 1995, while the number of establishments in manufacturing and construction both fell. These trends are apparent across Greater London as a whole, with the fall in the number of manufacturing establishments the most striking and highlights further the continuing process of

Figure 1: Census of Employment 1991 to 1995 - establishments (per cent)

Establishments, % of all			
	1991	1993	1995
Manufacturing	11.7	11.1	9.4
Construction	8.8	5.9	6.7
Distribution/Hotels/Restaurants	31	31.6	33.4
Transport/Comms	5	4.8	5
Finance/Business Serv	19.7	22.3	23.1
Public Sector	15.3	15	14.2
Other	8.2	8.7	7.8

Source: NOMIS/ONS, July 1997.

deindustrialisation as described in an earlier *Trends East* report (Rix, 1997). During the first half of the 1990s, London East and the LETEC area have seen their manufacturing base shrink by one quarter, 23.6 per cent and 23.0 per cent respectively. The comparable figure for London as a whole is one fifth or 19.0 per cent.

To understand more fully the dynamics of these changes it is important to look at establishments in terms of corporate structure and the degree of autonomy in decision-making. The location of strategic decision-making which affects establishments is determined by their 'control nature', i.e. whether they are independent single site firms, company headquarters which run their own establishment along with branch operations or subsidiary businesses, branches of headquarters, or non-commercial public sector organisations subject to statutory decisions.

The 1996 pan-London Employers Survey found that there is a slightly higher proportion (65 per cent) of single site establishments in the London East sub-region compared with Greater London as a whole (57 per cent, see Table 1), and a lower representation of headquarter sites, 10 per cent and 17 per cent respectively. Within London East, there is greater density of headquarters in the eastern fringe of the City and Docklands, with Tower Hamlets having a density of headquarters similar to the London average. Outer London boroughs on the north side of the river, such as Havering, Redbridge and Waltham Forest, have a greater concentration of single site establishments, which make up around three quarters of businesses in each borough.

Almost nine out of ten (89 per cent)

manufacturing establishments in London East are independent single site operations, compared with 60 per cent for service sector establishments. There are also, not surprisingly, considerable differences in the control status of establishments depending on their size. One quarter (25 per cent) of medium and large firms in London East are headquarters, while a higher proportion is also branches of larger corporate groups. One in every four medium and large firms are public sector establishments.

Although data for London East is not available for the survey conducted in 1994, figures for the LETEC area show little change in the control of status of firms over the past two years. The higher proportion of branch establishments shown in 1994 is a reflection of the exclusion of public sector establishments in the survey that year.

Multi-site organisations were asked where major decisions about the company's strategy and policy were taken. Around 60 per cent of London East establishments which form part of a larger group of companies indicated that they took all decisions at their own establishment and a further one fifth (20 per cent) stated that they mainly took decisions at their establishment. Multi-site manufacturing firms appear to have a lower degree of decision-making powers compared with service sector establishments. Large establishments meanwhile tend to share strategic

Table 1: Control nature of employers in London East (per cent)

	Single site	Headquarters	Branch	PS/Other
All establishments	65	10	4	21
Manufacturing sector	89	6	4	1
Service sector	60	11	4	25
1-24 employees	69	8	3	20
25-199 employees	33	25	9	33
200+ employees	30	29	9	32
LETEC 1996	63	10	4	23
LETEC 1994	67	14	16	3
London 1996	57	17	9	17
London 1994	60	12	22	6

Source: Pan-London Employer Survey 1996

decision-making powers with other units in their organisation, with only a third (35 per cent) of establishments with 200 or more staff taking all key decisions.

Decisions taken away from the establishment can be either in London, elsewhere in the UK or abroad. A higher than (London) average proportion of London East establishments have at least some key decisions taken elsewhere in London, although fewer are linked to overseas decision-making. Establishments in the manufacturing sector and those employing 200 or more people not only share more decision-making with external units, as mentioned above, but also are more likely to be affected by decisions taken outside of London. This diversity in the degree of autonomy and location of control affecting London East firms is important in relation to, firstly, their ability to respond to local economic factors and, secondly, the appropriate level at which support agencies can influence company decisions.

The other key characteristic of establishments in London East identified by the Employer Survey is the type of business activity conducted at the site, that is its 'function' within a wider corporate structure. In this sense, the survey focused on those private sector establishments, which were part of multi-site organisations.

Although a smaller proportion of London East establishments are designated as headquarters compared with London as a whole, the former are slightly more likely to perform some head-office type activities. This would suggest a lesser degree of functional specialisation amongst London East firms, with more workplaces having involvement in planning activities. Given the predominantly small size of local establishments a higher proportion also conducted sales and marketing and routine office functions.

What is more revealing regarding degrees of functional specialisation amongst London East multi-site establishments compared with London as a whole is what they stated as their *main* function or activity. Table 2 shows that similar proportions of establishments, both compared with London and across sectors, concentrate on head-office functions. More striking however is that only 24 per cent of multi-site manufacturing establishments in London East consider their main function to be manufacturing.

There is a negligible proportion of multi-site establishments specialising in design or research functions in London East, whether in manufacturing or services. This is a point of concern since this is likely to influence the dynamism of the local economy in terms of product innovation and company start-up potential.

Dynamics in the business base

The sectoral, control and functional characteristics of employer

Table 2: Main function of multi-site private sector establishments (per cent)

	London East			London
	All	Manu	Services	All
Head-office functions	33	27	31	27
Sales and marketing	31	21	33	23
Design or research	-	-	-	6
Delivery of services	11	2	12	21
Purchasing	2	-	3	1
Routine office	4	17	3	7
Logistics	9	-	10	3
Manufacturing/processing	2	24	1	3

Source: Pan-London Employer Survey 1996

organisations so far discussed provides a more static picture of businesses in the area. A key objective in conducting an annual survey however has been to assess changes in the business base and its commercial strengths, particularly in relation to the wider regional economy, which provides a benchmark for local firms. Reorganisation in the local economy is expected to continue throughout the nineties as businesses strive for optimum cost structures and profitability. The Employer Survey focuses on four key indicators:

- age distribution of establishments
- sales and market performance
- company restructuring
- relocation activity

These indicators are benchmarked below against data available from the 1994 survey across the LETEC are, and across London as a whole, to give an impression of the relative strengths and stability of firms in London East.

First however it is worth examining VAT registration figures for new businesses. Recent VAT registration data for London East, which in 1995 includes new firms with a turnover equal to or greater than of £45,000 per annum, shows a decline in most sectors and a 23 per cent fall overall (see Figure 2). The decline in the number of businesses registering for VAT between 1993 and 1995 is also evident for the LETEC area and London as a whole, albeit to a lesser degree, 12.5 per cent and 7.5 per cent respectively. This would suggest that firm formation is weaker in Hackney and south of the river and much stronger elsewhere in London.

The growth in 'other services' in London East, by 19.8 per cent between

1991 and 1995, is a positive sign of dynamism, although the sharp decline in finance and related registrations since 1993 is of concern.

The dynamism of a local economy can also be gauged by the *age distribution* of businesses. The London East employer base has a slightly older age profile compared with London as a whole (see Table 3). Only 2 per cent of establishments at the time of the survey were less than two years old whilst establishments that had been trading for over ten years make up almost 70 per cent of the total. While there is no clear causal relationship between firm registration rate and age of establishment, the above analysis supports the argument that London East has a lower firm formation rate than elsewhere in London.

Survey data reveal some divergence in the age profiles of establishments across the ten boroughs in London East. While four out of five establishments in Newham and Barking and Dagenham were established for over ten years, one third of establishments in the outer London boroughs of Havering and Redbridge had been trading between three and ten years. 1994 Employer Survey figures for the LETEC area and London show considerably higher proportions of younger establishments than compared with 1996. This is confirmed by the fall in the number of firms registering for VAT, as discussed above.

Figure 2: VAT registrations 1991 to 1995

VAT registrations	1991	1993	1995
Construction	840	800	970
Manufacturing	1230	1110	895
Transport	440	335	360
Wholesale/Retail	2750	2700	2020
Finance & Related	600	555	100
Other Services	1990	1840	2385
	1991	1993	1995
Thames Gateway	8492	7396	6563
LETEC	4516	4311	3951
London	36207	36382	33481

Source: NOMIS/ONS, July 1997

The second indicator of business dynamism addressed by the Employer Survey is *sales and market performance*. In contrast to the general climate of low business confidence in Britain in the early 1990s, both the 1994 and 1996 surveys show a generally up-beat response from local employers. Table 4 shows the percentage of firms reporting increases or decreases in sales or output in the 12 months prior to the survey. Over half (56 per cent) of the establishments in London East reported some degree of growth, compared with 14 per cent which experienced a fall in sales or output. The sub-regional trend is not as pronounced as that at the London level, where the net number of establishments reporting growth leapt from 27 per cent to 57 per cent. There is continuing relative weakness in manufacturing establishments in London East, with a worrying 13 per cent of respondents reporting declines in output or sales of over 10 per cent.

Small and medium-sized enterprises (SMEs) are being seen as the principal source of growth in the economy in the 1990s. The 1996 survey found however that higher proportions of medium-sized rather than the small establishments reported at least moderate growth and fewer reported a decline in output or sales.

Two fifths (40 per cent) of London East establishments surveyed in 1996 regarded the market in which they are operating, regardless of their own performance, as being fairly stable. A comparable figure was evident for

Table 3: Age of establishments in the London East (per cent)

	<2 years years	3 to 10 years	over 10 years
All establishments	2	27	69
Manufacturing sector	2	26	73
Service sector	3	27	68
1-24 employees	2	27	69
25-199 employees	2	27	70
200+ employees	-	13	82
LETEC 1996	3	25	70
LETEC 1994	10	22	68
London 1996	5	32	63
London 1994	12	33	55

Source: Pan-London Employer Survey 1996

Table 4: London East establishments reporting changes in sales/output (%)

	Up 10%+	Up <10%	Down <10%	Down 10%+	Net difference
All establishments	35	21	8	6	+42
Manufacturing sector	36	16	10	13	+29
Service sector	35	23	7	5	+46
1-24 employees	35	20	8	6	+41
25-199 employees	35	29	4	2	+58
200+ employees	37	24	6	-	+55
LETEC 1996	31	21	8	6	+38
LETEC 1994	28	18	8	6	+32
London 1996	43	22	5	3	+57
London 1994	43		16		+27

Source: Pan-London Employer Survey 1996

London as a whole. Significantly lower proportions of firms in the subregion say they operate in growth markets however, and slightly more operate in declining ones compared with the London average. Manufacturing establishments again stand out in the survey as those generally at risk of under-performing; almost one in every ten admits to be surviving in markets that are declining strongly.

In order to stem the continuing decline in manufacturing, local firms will need to alter their product profile and structure in order to compete effectively in growth markets. Medium and large establishments in the London East subregion appear to be in a safer position, with similar proportions to the London average operating in growth markets.

Evidence of firms responding to either market difficulties or new growth opportunities was found in survey analysis of *organisational restructuring and changes in ownership* amongst London East establishments. One fifth of establishments had either restructured or changed hands in the two years prior to the survey. This finding was consistent across all sectors and with the recent London trend, although there is some variation among the boroughs. A higher incidence of organisational restructuring and changes in ownership was found amongst medium and large establishments however. While this might suggest greater dynamism among medium and large establishments, it is more likely to be the product of greater organisational flexibility and take-over desirability of larger enterprises.

The fourth dynamic in the business base addressed by the Employer Survey is *relocation activity*. Analysis of survey findings is augmented by Prism Research LTD's CREDO database, which tracks business movements around the country. There was a marginal net out-flow of firms from the London East boroughs in the LETEC area in the twelve months prior to the survey, with losses in construction, engineering and other manufacturing and gains in business and financial services. The other significant trend revealed by the CREDO database is that net gains in firm relocations to the East London sub-region are offset by net losses out to Essex and other satellite locations of the capital.

However, the 1996 Employer Survey revealed that only one in ten (10 per cent) establishments had definite intentions to relocate from their present site and a further 17 per cent indicated that relocation was a possibility. This is broadly in line with London-wide trends and slightly down on the intentions stated in the 1994 survey. A higher proportion of manufacturing establishments are considering moving away from their present location; the main reasons of those definitely planning to move are expansion of premises, modernisation of operations and skills deficiencies in the present workforce. In contrast almost 80 per cent of service sector establishments definitely planning to relocate said either larger or better quality premises were the main reasons for moving.

There is a challenge therefore for London East to improve retention within the subregion of those establishments planning to relocate, which the survey reveals to be moving for positive reasons. Sixty per cent of London East establishments with intentions to relocate would prefer to stay within their immediate borough and another 34 per cent within Greater London. This is common practice amongst retail/wholesale and other small-scale service sector businesses, however manufacturing and large establishments are more likely to relocate further afield with almost 40 per cent of the former seeking locations outside London but within the south-east.

Corporate linkages and strategies

Customer and Supplier Bases

The nature of an establishment's *customer base* is clearly important to the prospects for the establishment itself and, in aggregate, to the local economy. This report has already examined the performance of individual establishments, in terms of sales or output, and employers' perceptions about the markets in

Table 5: Geography of customer base (per cent)

	Local	London	SE	UK	EU	Other Overseas
All establishments	84	90	79	62	35	30
Manufacturing sector	82	93	85	74	53	33
Service sector	84	89	77	62	35	32
1-24 employees	84	90	78	61	33	29
25-199 employees	80	90	83	74	50	41
200+ employees	84	89	86	80	52	52
LETEC all firms	87	91	80	62	34	31
London all firms	82	88	78	70	47	44

Source: Pan-London Employer Survey 1996

which they operate. This section will now look at the geographical distribution of markets and types of customers.

In addition, the distribution of an establishment's *supplier networks* can profoundly influence the links a firm has with the local economy in which it is located. This in turn will influence the extent to which an establishment is dependent upon the performance of the local or regional economy, or particular local sectors, rather than national or international trends. By identifying the profile of supplier networks, and the changing trends in such networks, the Employer Survey provides some indications of the inter-dependence of different local firms with the economic environment in which they operate.

Looking at customer bases first of all, Table 5 shows that more than four fifths (84 per cent) of establishments in London East have highly localised markets; that is, within three miles of their establishment. The majority of establishments also sell to markets across London and the South East in general, 90 per cent and 79 per cent respectively. As the distance increases away from the establishment the proportion of firms selling to such markets decreases, to the extent that only one third (35 per cent) of establishments in London East export at least some of their products or services to the European Union (EU) and 30 per cent to other countries overseas. The comparable figures for establishments in London as a whole are 47 per cent and 44 per cent. Fewer than one in ten (9 per cent) establishments in London identified

Table 6: Types of customers of London East Establishments (per cent)

	Ind./ consumers	Distrib/ commercial	Retailers wholesalers	Public sector	Domestic consumers	Internal div.s
All establishments	76	38	41	55	55	4
Manufacturing sector	89	55	43	65	44	2
Service sector	73	37	41	51	57	4
1-24 employees	76	37	41	55	56	3
25-199 employees	72	42	43	51	47	11
200+ employees	71	34	30	59	51	15
LETEC all firms	74	36	37	50	54	4
London all firms	69	34	39	45	49	4

Source: Pan-London Employer Survey 1996

the EU as their main market (3 per cent for establishments in London East).

15 per cent of establishments in London East reported that their main market was within 3 miles of their establishment. With regard to the six LETEC boroughs, establishments involved in real estate, renting and business services together with wholesale and retail firms, were characterised by the most localised markets. Of these establishments, 23 per cent and 21 per cent, respectively, indicated that their main market was within three miles of their establishment.

While one third (32 per cent) of establishments in London East stated that proximity to customers was not important, 48 per cent considered proximity to be either important or very important. Small establishments were generally more likely than medium or large firms to regard proximity to customers as important. When asked about the changing importance of London as a customer base, 18 per cent of establishments reported that London had become more important, while 16 per cent stated that London had become less important. The majority (57 per cent) of establishments in London East did not identify any change in the importance of London as a customer base.

Around three quarters of establishments in London East (76 per cent) and the LETEC area (74 per cent) and 69 per cent of establishments in London as a whole supply goods or services direct to other firms in industry or commerce (see Table 6). A smaller proportion, 55 per

Table 7: Geography of supplier base (per cent)

	London	Sth East	UK	EU	Overseas
All establishments	64	61	66	25	20
Manufacturing sector	68	73	77	29	24
Service sector	62	57	62	25	21
1-24 employees	63	61	66	24	19
25-199 employees	71	67	65	29	21
200+ employees	67	66	68	44	34
LETEC all firms	67	65	70	26	20
London all firms	64	53	62	29	26

Source: Pan-London Employer Survey 1996

cent, 54 per cent and 49 per cent respectively, sell direct to the general public. As one would expect, medium and large firms were relatively more likely to supply goods or services to other divisions within their organisation, 11 per cent and 15 per cent, respectively, compared with 3 per cent for small establishments.

In terms of *supplier networks*, the Employer Survey indicates that two thirds (64 per cent) of establishments across London source at least some of their materials, components or services from within Greater London (see Table 7). No more than one quarter of establishments in London East, three in ten establishments for London as a whole, extend their supplier networks beyond the UK. Again, the survey results highlight the reliance of establishments in London East, and London in general, on domestic markets.

One quarter (25 per cent) of establishments in London East identified their main supplier base as London. The comparable figures for the LETEC area and London as a whole are 22 per cent and 28 per cent.

While more than half (51 per cent) of establishments across London reported that proximity to suppliers was not important, around one fifth (21 per cent) regard proximity to suppliers to be either important or very important. More than 70 per cent of establishments in London East reported no change in the importance of proximity to suppliers.

Local regeneration partnerships and business support agencies place considerable importance on developing local supply chains. Survey

Table 8: Adequacy of technology and equipment (per cent)

	More than	OK	Less than	Not factor
All establishments	38	47	10	4
Manufacturing sector	29	58	9	4
Service sector	38	46	10	5
1-24 employees	38	47	10	4
25-199 employees	35	51	11	2
200+ employees	47	46	7	-
LETEC all firms	40	43	12	5
London all firms	43	42	10	5

Source: Pan-London Employer Survey 1996

results highlight the scale of the problem likely to be encountered, with only one quarter of establishments in London East seeing Greater London as their main supplier base and only one in five regarding proximity to suppliers to be important.

Innovation and Product Development

The ability of firms to compete effectively is increasingly intertwined with their ability to keep pace with rapidly changing technological advances. Private sector employers were asked to comment on the adequacy of their current technology and equipment in relation to current output levels. Table 8 shows that around two fifths (38 per cent) of private sector establishments in the London East regard their technology and equipment to be more than adequate for their needs. However, a significant minority (10 per cent) indicated that their technology and equipment was inadequate for their current needs and thus, was likely to be constraining output. Similar findings are evident for the LETEC area and London as a whole.

Establishments were also asked to comment on the importance of product or service innovation. Just over three fifths (61 per cent) of private sector establishments in London East recognise the need to innovate as being important or very important. Large establishments tend to attach greater importance to the need for innovation, but this can be partly explained by their greater capacity to undertake such developments. Around one in ten private sector establishments in London East (12 per cent) and London as a whole (11 per cent)

Table 9: *Planning or Managerial Tools Adopted in London East (per cent)*

	Business plan/ Corporate strategy	Quality control procedures	Sales forecasting	Cash sales forecasts	Management accounts	Formal staff involvement	Recruitment plan	Staff development plan	Equal Opportunities policy
All establishments	44	58	53	67	84	49	20	38	39
Manufacturing sector	43	76	52	70	86	47	14	39	25
Service sector	44	54	54	69	82	50	21	39	39
1-24 employees	42	57	51	66	83	47	17	35	36
25-199 employees	69	71	70	80	88	61	43	61	57
200+ employees	81	82	79	78	96	75	71	80	82
LETEC all firms	42	54	53	63	79	49	19	37	37
London all firms	53	57	62	73	85	55	31	42	45

Source: Pan-London Employer Survey 1996

however did not consider product or service innovation to be at all important.

Recognition of the importance of product or service innovation was not always matched by actual practice. When asked if their establishment had significantly extended or developed its products or services in the two years prior to the survey, only four in ten (43 per cent) private sector establishments indicated that they had. Nearly half (49 per cent) of the establishments surveyed in London overall reported that they had developed their products or services in the two years prior to the survey. One third (36 per cent) of private sector establishments across London also indicated that they had undertaken process or technological innovation, 50 per cent for medium and large establishments in London East.

Management and Quality Systems

In terms of managerial or planning tools, establishments in London East are more likely to have in place regular management accounts (89 per cent), regular cash sales forecasts (67 per cent) and systematic quality control procedures (58 per cent), with the latter more common in manufacturing establishments (76 per cent, see Table 9). Larger differences are however evident between different sizes of establishment, with the proportions for those establishments using each managerial or planning tool being greater for large and medium establishments than for small establishments.

The development of high quality products and services lies at the heart of any strategy to achieve and sustain increasing levels of competitiveness. It is now becoming more common for suppliers to produce evidence, which shows that steps to ensure consistent quality are in place. The Employer Survey therefore investigated the local penetration of four principal quality systems; namely, BS5750/ISO9000, Total Quality Management (TQM), the 'environmental' standard BS7750 and the Investors in People (IiP) standard.

Around one fifth (22 per cent) of establishments in London East were committed to or accredited with BS5750/ISO9000 at the time of the survey, and 11 per cent IiP. One in twenty (6 per cent) establishments were committed to or accredited with TQM. The comparable figure for the environment standard was only 1 per cent. Similar findings were evident for the LETEC area and London as a whole. Large firms were generally more likely than SMEs to have been committed to or accredited with any these quality systems at the time of the survey.

Human resource implications

The dynamics in the London East business base and corporate strategies pursued in establishments in order to maintain long term competitiveness have major implications for human resource requirements and the labour market. Recent years have seen a trend towards greater flexibility of employment, with nearly one quarter of UK employees employed on a part time or temporary basis. A recent study for the TECs and LECs (Local Enterprise Companies in Scotland) concluded that permanent jobs tended to be lost in older sectors whilst new flexible employment was more commonplace among service industries (Business Strategies Ltd 1996).

This trend in workforce structures has particular benefits for many employers and for some employees. It also underlines how the world of work is changing rapidly and, in particular, how employment is becoming less stable. People change jobs much more frequently than they used to and whole career changes are now more common. This growing instability in the workplace implies the need for much greater workforce adaptability and the need to be able to learn new skills as jobs change. This places the *skill levels* of a business's workforce, particularly the ability of workers to *learn new skills,* as central factors in determining business competitiveness.

In order to identify how some of these issues manifest themselves in the context of the London East economy, and to describe some of the different approaches towards human resource management adopted by London East employers, the Employer Survey asked about:

- Underskilling;
- Vacancies and recruitment;
- Training strategies of London East employers.

Changes in the London East Workforce

It can be seen from Figure 3, that the workforce of London East during the first half of the 1990s shrunk by 4.8 per cent, marginally higher than that for the LETEC area (-4.3 per cent) but more than twice that experienced by London as a whole (-1.9 per cent). The sectors suffering the greatest falls in employment in London East are manufacturing (17,409), public administration, education and health (13,513) and construction (8,850). The only two sectors not to experience a fall in the level of employment are banking, finance and insurance, and distribution, hotels and restaurants, with gains of 9.0 per cent and 3.1 per cent respectively.

The findings of the Employer Survey however point to a slight upturn in fortunes for London East. In the 12 months prior to the survey, 30 per cent of establishments experienced an increase in the size of their workforce, nearly half (48 per cent) had seen no change and 15 per cent reported a declining workforce (see Table 10). While small employers were more likely to have reported no change in the size of their workforce,

Figure 3, Census of Employment 1991 to 1995 - employees

	1991	1993	1995
Manufact	4,671	4,228	3,566
Construc	3,513	2,247	2,542
Distributi	12,376	12,036	12,671
Transport	1,996	1,828	1,897
Fin/Bus	7,864	8,494	8,764
Public	6,108	5,713	5,387
Other	3,274	3,314	2,959
	London E	**LETEC**	**London**
Manufact	-19.6	-23.5	-16.4
Construc	-28.6	-23.4	-25.2
Distributi	3.1	4	6.1
Transport	-3.5	1	-11.9
Banking	9	10.8	9.5
Public ad	-7.8	-8.5	-7.7
Other ser	-3.8	-2.5	3.5
All indust	-4.8	-4.3	-1.9

Source: NOMIS/ONS, July 1997. (*Includes agriculture and fishing, and energy and water).

Table 10: Employment change

	Increase	No Change	Decrease	Net difference
All establishments	30	48	15	+15
Manufacturing sector	26	51	13	+13
Service sector	30	48	15	+15
1-24 employees	20	60	18	+2
25-199 employees	44	37	15	+29
200+ employees	41	49	10	+31
LETEC 1996	23	53	20	+3
LETEC 1994	29	52	17	+12
London 1996	29	52	16	+13

Source: London TECs 1996 Employer Survey

no noticeable difference is evident between the manufacturing and service sector establishments. Establishments in the LETEC area have faired relatively poorly compared with those in London East as a whole, and demonstrate less growth and more decline than the survey in 1994 identified.

Independent of workforce change, establishments were asked to assess the changes in productivity in the twelve months prior to the survey. Two fifths (41 per cent) of establishments stated that productivity had increased, fewer than one in ten (9 per cent) reported a fall in the level of productivity. Manufacturing establishments were more bullish with just over 50 per cent reporting productivity increases.

To compete effectively in the marketplace, companies need a workforce which is properly equipped with the specific skills needed for production and service delivery. The environment in which companies operate is not static, requiring workers to upgrade existing skills or reskill to meet new challenges.

Establishments were asked to identify whether any members of their staff were not as highly skilled as they would like. While 73 per cent of establishments identified no skills deficiencies in their current staff, one in four (25 per cent) did report skills shortages. Large establishments (37 per cent) were more likely to identify workers with skills deficiencies, but this is not surprising considering their larger workforce. Manufacturing establishments reporting skills deficiencies targeted craft and operative employees, while those in the service sector identified clerical and sales employees.

The above analysis is somewhat oversimplified as it gives little idea of how widespread skill deficiencies are within an establishment that has identified a skill deficiency problem among existing staff. In addition, the skills shortages suffered by employers do not always result in a loss of business or earnings. The most commonly cited impacts of these shortages is an increase of pressure on other staff (58 per cent of establishments reporting this as an outcome), a loss of quality (45 per cent), a loss of output (41 per cent) and a loss of sales (37 per cent). Manufacturing establishments were twice as likely as service sector establishments to report late delivery as a consequence of skills shortages, 47 per cent and 19 per cent respectively.

Recruitment and skill shortages

Reflecting the predominance of small firms in London East and London generally, the majority (51 per cent) of establishments interviewed stated that they prefer to recruit locally. A further 16 per cent of establishments sourced their recruitment from across London. One quarter (23 per cent) of establishments search on a national and/or international basis for the right staff. It is likely that the breadth of search for employees is a reflection of the level of specialism these occupations represent.

Of those establishments which reported vacancies at the time of the survey, 57 per cent had at least some which were 'hard to fill' (see Table 11). Hard to fill vacancies were less likely to have been reported by establishments in the manufacturing sector (47 per cent) than service sector establishments (56 per cent). In terms of size of establishment, those employing 24 or fewer workers appear more likely to experience problems when recruiting. Twice as many small establishments identified recruitment problems than their counterparts employing 200 or more people, 65 per cent and 30 per cent respectively.

Table 11: Establishments with hard to fill vacancies

	Yes	No
All establishments	57	43
Manufacturing sector	47	53
Service sector	56	44
1-24 employees	65	35
25-199 employees	44	56
200+ employees30	70	
LETEC all firms	59	41
London all firms	50	50

Source: London TECs 1996 Employer Survey

London East (and the LETEC area) has only a marginally higher percentage of establishments with hard to fill vacancies than that for London as a whole.

The reasons why establishments have problems recruiting are again wide and varied, but the most commonly cited are 'applicants lacked suitable skills' (14 per cent), 'applicants lacked personal qualities' (13 per cent) and 'a lack of skilled applicants' (12 per cent). Manufacturing firms are far more likely to have faced a 'lack of any applicants', 45 per cent compared with 7 per cent of service sector establishments. This would point to the problems being faced by manufacturing establishments being significantly different both in terms of skill deficiencies, recruitment problems and the effect these then have upon the operation of the firm. One quarter (25 per cent) of large establishments with hard to fill vacancies perceived applicants to lack the relevant experience, only 2 per cent identified 'a lack of skilled applicants' as the problem.

Training Practices

Given that many firms identified training and recruitment problems, it would be reasonable to find remedial measures being undertaken by firms. While it is not possible in this report to cross reference those establishments offering training against those with training and recruitment problems, it

Table 12: Training by type and proportion of workforce

	On-the-job only	Off-the-job only	Both types	None	Up to half	Over half
All establishments	32	8	34	24	29	47
Manufacturing sector	50	3	23	24	45	31
Service sector	30	8	36	25	27	48
1-24 employees	33	9	30	27	28	45
25-199 employees	27	4	64	5	26	69
200+ employees	9	-	87	2	32	66
LETEC 1996	32	9	32	26	39	30
LETEC 1994	30	3	46	21	N/A	N/A
London 1996	30	6	40	22	35	34

Source: London TECs 1996 Employer Survey

might seem surprising that one firm in four (24 per cent) stated that they trained none of their staff. However, this figure should not be taken as the exact measure of training activity in the economy, some element that one company might openly recognise as another might not consider staff training.

In the twelve months prior to the survey, almost half (47 per cent) of the establishments claim to have provided training for over half of their workforce (see Table 12). Unsurprisingly access to training is related to size of firm. Only 2 per cent of establishments with 200 or more employees do not carry out any training of employees, compared with 27 per cent of small establishments. One third (32 per cent) of establishments only carried out on-the-job training, while a further 34 per cent carried out both on- and off-the-job training. Comparable figures are evident for the LETEC area and London as a whole.

Thirty per cent of establishments reported that the level of training carried out at their establishment had increased in the 12 months prior to the survey, as opposed to the 2 per cent that had reported a decline.

With the exception of induction and IT training, the main types of training undertaken by employers in London East are related to Health and Safety procedures (58 per cent), the installation of new equipment (57 per cent), and the introduction of new products or services (57 per cent). One third of establishments carried out management (31 per cent) and/or supervisory (32 per cent) training, and 39 per cent training related to professional development.

Just over one quarter (28 per cent) of those employees receiving some kind of training was awarded a formal qualification. There is therefore an evident need to improve the quality of training or, at least, to improve the system of accreditation and facilitate the transferability of skills.

At the time of the survey, 29 per cent of establishments in the London East area had a designated budget for training, 27 per cent a training officer, 26 per cent an establishment-wide training policy and nearly half (48 per cent) carried out some form of evaluation of the training undertaken (see Table 13). The incidence of each of these is higher in service sector establishments and those employing 25 or more people.

In summary, larger establishments have much better human resource practices than their smaller counterparts, that of course is no surprise, the interesting comparison is the scale of the difference. Larger firms have both greater resources to fund training and the better structure to cope with the loss of productive capability. The question of most importance is how these percentages vary over time, where comparisons can be made the LETEC part of the London East has not made significant

Table 13: How training is organised

	Designated budget	Training officer	Central planning	Evaluation systems
All establishments	29	27	26	48
Manufacturing sector	11	14	9	39
Service sector	34	29	29	51
1-24 employees	25	23	22	45
25-199 employees	50	50	49	63
200+ employees	76	72	68	80
LETEC 1996	27	26	25	44
LETEC 1994	41	44	46	54
London 1996	35	29	32	43

Source: London TECs 1996 Employer Survey

progress.

Policy conclusions

While most establishments recognise the importance of innovation to continued market competitiveness, a lower proportion (40 per cent) had actually developed products or services and 35 per cent had undertaken some form of process or technological innovation. Results from the Employer Survey also point to particular difficulties faced by small establishments in keeping pace with product service, process and technological development, and adopting a strategic approach to financial, human resource and other managerial procedures. Small establishments are often least able to devote the time and resources necessary to such practices and developments. It is imperative for the future dynamism of the London East economy that training and business support agencies assist small companies in meeting these challenges.

There is a relatively high degree of autonomy over decision-making among local businesses, although less for manufacturing establishments. This suggests that London East is not heavily vulnerable to external corporate decisions. Support to local businesses can therefore be targeted at local managers who in turn will have the necessary autonomy to respond.

The erosion of London's manufacturing base, which is projected to continue into the next millennium, creates particular challenges if the range and number of local employment opportunities are to be sustained. Although employment in the service sector will continue to increase, the extent that this will simply reflect a transfer from full to part-time opportunities remains unclear. A shift from manufacturing jobs to high quality service sector jobs also presents challenges to local employers and support agencies.

Since customer and supplier networks among London East establishments are shown to be fairly diverse, the potential for local supply chain initiatives is limited. The customer base of London East firms is to a large degree dependent on the domestic UK economy. There is a need therefore to encourage greater market diversification in overseas markets, where currently only 35 per cent of establishments export to the EU and 30 per cent further overseas.

Although the demand for labour among local businesses remain relatively depressed, a minority of establishments experienced problems in filling certain vacancies and/or identified skills deficiencies among existing members of staff. There appears to have been a marginal increase in the number of establishments, and their commitment towards, carrying out training of employees in London East, but a significant minority (24 per cent), predominantly small establishments, undertook no training at the time of the survey. These findings highlight the need to continue to encourage local employers to increase their overall commitment to workforce training and their capacity to deliver such training.

Human resource development should be central to any organisations thinking with respect to future competitiveness. Employers are continually placing increased demands upon their workforce, seeking a higher level of ability and understanding for jobs that previously required a lesser degree of capability. An ever-advancing technological base is breaking down the occupational hierarchy between professional, technical and operation occupations. Employers and employees must both commit themselves to managing this period of change and develop the skills needed in the workforce during the next millennium.

REFERENCES

Business Strategies Ltd, (1996) *Flexible Employment: Implications for TECs and LECs*, first report, May.

London TECs, (1996) *An Economic Profile of London*, a report by London Training and Enterprise Councils.

London TECs, (1997) *London Employers Survey 1996-97*, a report by Prism Research Ltd for the London Training and Enterprise Councils.

Rix, V., (1997) 'Industrial decline, economic restructuring and social exclusion in London East, 1980s and 1990s', *Rising East*, Volume 1 Number 1, p118-41.

NOTES

1. Became known as the Annual Employment Survey in 1995.

2. There are now seven London TECs, following the merger earlier this year of Central London TEC and Central and Inner London North TEC

ARTY FACTS

Bread and circuses?

The making of Hoxton's cultural quarter and its impact on urban regeneration in Hackney

Andrew Attfield

In 1993 parts of Hoxton and Shoreditch were included in Hackney's City Challenge area, the Dalston City Corridor, and projects based there have subsequently played a major role in the local regeneration strategy. This article considers the part played by regeneration activity in forming a 'cultural quarter' in Hoxton, and the role of cultural industries in Shoreditch as a whole. I look at the ways in which this has come about, and what impact the 'cultural quarter' has had on the regeneration programme, the business community and the local community. Then I move on to discuss what role the cultural industries can and should play in regeneration activity and to the arguments around how important they are in regard to the wider economy.

At a time when 'cultural quarters' appear to be springing up like mushrooms in British cities, this local case study tries to come to conclusions as to how significant the formation of such quarters and related business sectors are to urban regeneration. One key issue that will arise throughout the article is what is meant by a 'cultural quarter'?. The largely economic strategy and criteria employed when assessing the projects comprising the quarter have competed with a host of other perceptions of what is implied by the process, including concerns that the evening economy was being unduly emphasised, or that a fashionable residential district was being created that would price out existing communities and businesses.

Much of the complexities in this can be seen in the historical development of Shoreditch, to which we initially turn.

Dalston City Challenge Area

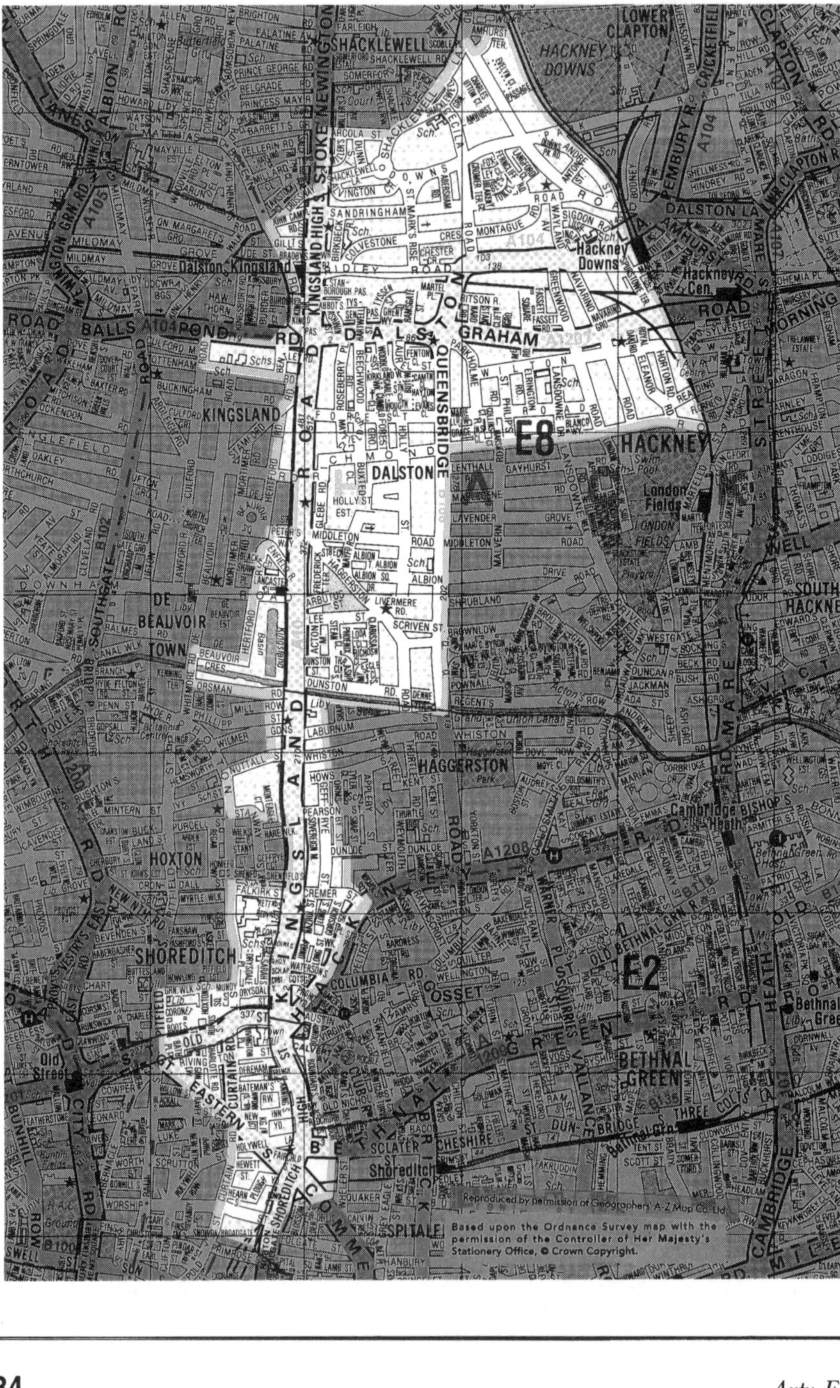

History

Hoxton is one of the historic districts lying to the north of the City of London. It forms part of Shoreditch, which was incorporated in the London Borough of Hackney in 1963. Shoreditch has not wanted for culture. In the Elizabethan period, it was the location for London's first theatres, 'The Theatre' and the 'The Curtain'. Curtain Road EC2, one of the main thoroughfares in Shoreditch, recalls this connection. Shakespeare acted here; Christopher Marlowe lived (and duelled) in Shoreditch High Street; Richard Burbage, the actor/impresario is buried in Shoreditch Church. In more recent times the area was a centre for music hall, and one of its greatest stars, Marie Lloyd, was Hoxton born. Gainsborough Studios was located in Hoxton, and Alfred Hitchcock, amongst many others, worked there.

In the late nineteenth century, Shoreditch was a focus of the furniture trade, mainly located in small workshops. It also had a substantial clothing manufacturing industry, and significant employment in printing and publishing. With the removal of manufacturing to the Lee Valley and beyond in the 1950s and 1960s, the main employment uses in Shoreditch came to be those related to City support industries (professional, business and operational services). In the 1980s, the explosion in financial services led to substantial pressure for new office space, which resulted in a number of major developments in the south of the area, most obviously, the Broadgate Development.

On the whole, the transformation of the local economy has not benefited local people. The new jobs in financial and City support services have not been taken in the main by local people, whose skills and expectations related to industries that were redundant or gone from the area. Despite the massive transformations taking place around Shoreditch, Hoxton remained in many ways a traditional working-class community. Levels of unemployment hit new heights during the recession of the early 1980s and have remained high. As a result, the local authority began to consider means of addressing this issue in the late 1980s by instigating employment and training programmes for local people to enable them to access the City job market. But this was a difficult process. The City job market is a regional one, attracting workers from all over the South East, as well as London, and often requiring educational and skill attainments beyond the scope of many local people. Hackney's large black and ethnic population were disadvantaged by language issues as well as by racism, in what is still an overwhelmingly white labour force. On top of these difficulties, the recession of the late 1980s and early 1990s and restructuring in the financial services led to a substantial reduction in employment and a collapse in property prices. In any case, the prosperity evident in Shoreditch had never quite made it into Hoxton, lapping tidal-like on the southern shores of Old Street.

The opportunities of recession

The growth of the mid-1980s led to a spiral in office accommodation costs in Shoreditch. Developers looked at Broadgate and foresaw this kind of development creeping further north into Shoreditch. As a result, the recession left many developers and freeholders with wildly unrealistic book values. This followed the previous, even deeper, market collapse of the early 1970s, and the accumulative effect was to leave a number of sites derelict and buildings derelict. In addition, a number of sites owned by Hackney Council to the north of Old Street remained undeveloped, although a good deal of groundwork had been covered by the council through projects funded by the South Shoreditch Improvement Area and the Urban Programme, including site assembly and property improvement.

However, despite the overlying air of neglect, there were a number of regeneration opportunities for, despite the growth in financial and auxiliary services, Shoreditch remained full of surprises. Workshops survived from its previous history, whilst a limited number of artist's studios and galleries were emerging. Planning policy for the area had attempted to retain employment uses where possible, and had, in the main successfully retained the stock of attractive eighteenth century factory and warehouse buildings. However, following 20 years of attempting unsuccessfully to retain industrial employment in the area, the council had been ordered to adopt a more flexible approach to changes in use. A small number of residential or live and work permissions were granted, leading to a local population evolving which was centred on the arts and cultural industries. These were supplemented by a number of residential habitations of studio spaces. A jazz club, the Bass Clef, had been operational since 1983. Hence there was a sense of a bohemian culture arising in the area, which seemed to be worth consideration from the point of view of developing a cultural/media economy and in terms of attracting visitors. Given the relative absence of other economic growth potential at the time, this seemed the most obvious option. This approach was also complementary to the other regeneration activities initiated by the City Challenge programme, Dalston City Partnership (DCP), including the construction of Hackney Community College's Shoreditch campus (a 6,000 student strong new development on the site of the old Shoreditch School) and a wide range of training and employment initiatives, environmental improvements and business support programmes.

Hoxton Square

Hoxton Square lies between the main Shoreditch business district to the south, and the mainly residential area of Hoxton to the north. Despite its inherent attractiveness in terms of layout and much of its architecture, the square was partially derelict in the early 1990s. One side of the square was mainly derelict; and further west on Hoxton Market (no longer used as a street market) a number of sites remained unused. These included a large builder's yard; a bomb site that used to be a public baths (and was set aside for housing); a strip of land to the north of Old Street, used for advertising hoardings and car parking; and the former Shoreditch Power Station. This was an impressive set of industrial buildings dating from the Edwardian era, which had housed the first power station to burn domestic waste in London, but had been used as a council depot since 1945. Just to the north on Pitfield Street was Shoreditch Public Library, a Grade II listed Passmore Edwards Library, which was threatened with imminent redundancy. These sites together made up a significant set of lands, all in local authority ownership.

The first steps towards the regeneration of the square predated the City Challenge programme. A local developer, Glasshouse Investments Ltd, which specialises in studio space for arts and craft industries, purchased the derelict buildings fronting Hoxton Square and was assisted through the Urban Programme to refurbish these for artists' studios. This work was completed in the period 1991-93, and proved to be a success, leading to full occupancy. The City Challenge programme included three additional projects to build on this. The builder's yard was to be sold to Westminster University for student housing (developed by Greater London Enterprises), with City Challenge Grant contributing to the environmental enhancement of Hoxton Market. The former public baths was developed for housing by Shian Housing Association, funded through the Housing Corporation. Most significantly, the Shoreditch Power Station was set aside for occupation by Circus Space.

Circus Space

Circus Space is a circus school and cabaret venue originally based in

North Street, Islington, in property rented from United Workspace. It had outgrown its current accommodation to the extent that trainee trapeze artists had to swing out of the building through a hole in the wall. The Shoreditch Power Station was ideal for their needs. The ex-generating chamber suited the existing needs of the organisation, and there was space for smaller training studios and offices. Other parts of the site offered scope for improvement as space to be let to cultural industries and, as the *pièce de résistance*, the ex-incinerating chamber, cathedral-like in size, offered the opportunity for a performing arts venue, with height enough to satisfy the most ambitious trapeze artist.

The decision to run with Circus Space was not taken without debate. The factors that counted in its favour were that:

- it fitted in with the growing awareness of cultural industries in the borough (reinforced at the time by feasibility work commissioned by the council) .
- it was in line with the demand for property from cultural industry sectors.
- it seemed to offer tangible economic outputs in terms of new jobs being brought to the area and in terms of positive impact of new visitors on neighbouring visitors.
- it was an exciting project that enlivened the City Challenge proposal.

Despite the risks of supporting a project with financial support only guaranteed for its first phase, the Circus Space has amply repaid the regeneration investment made. It secured resources from the European Community Objective 2 sources and from the City Corporation for its second phase. It currently has a substantial Lottery bid in preparation for the third and final phase of the scheme which would bring the ex-incinerating chamber into use as a venue and rehearsal space. The project is an exemplar of how the not-for-profit sector can access private sector support using business leadership teams (in this case East London Partnership).

Just as importantly, the move of Circus Space into Hoxton showed that the arts and culture agenda was alive and attracted attention to the area.

The Blue Note

At the same time as Circus Space was commencing the improvement of its first phase, the Bass Clef was bought out by Acid Jazz Records Ltd. Acid Jazz is a leading independent record company, and their investment in the club was welcomed, especially since the previous owner had become bankrupt and there was a danger of the club slipping back into dereliction. The company was given a small grant from the business improvement grant regime to encourage it to refurbish the property and upgrade its recording studios. The ex-Bass Clef (renamed the 'Blue Note') specialised in dance music rather than the live acts promoted by the previous owner. This was often highly contemporary and gave the area a high and fashionable profile. However it became a focal point for community concern in regard to the transformation of the area (see below).

The Lux

Circus Space and the construction of the Westminster University student housing had already begun to transform the area by March 1994. By this time another project had come along which had been unforeseen in the original plan. This related to the derelict and largely vacant site at 2 - 4 Hoxton Square, which was in private ownership and lay between the Blue Note, Circus Space and Glasshouse's studios at 5 and 6 Hoxton Square. This was bought by Glasshouse to protect their existing holdings. Through discussion with the council's arts and leisure officers, DCP became aware of the need for two agencies funded through the British Film Institute to find joint office accommodation and other facilities. These were the London Video Agency (later

Lux Building, Hoxton Square. Photograph © Hèlène Binet

ENO Works, 40 Pitfield Street. Photograph Sue Adler ©ENO

renamed London Electronic Arts) and the London Film Makers' Co-operative, who fall under the umbrella of the London Film and Video Development Agency (LFVDA). In discussion with LFVDA, it became clear that there was a possible fit between the needs of the two agencies and the Glasshouse site. The two agencies would occupy approximately half the site, including a 200 seat cinema and a bespoke video gallery, with the remainder being let out to other media related industries.

It helped that Glasshouse had made a speciality of arts businesses and were already the freeholders. However it was evident that the project would require significant public sector support if it was to become viable. Following a lengthy process of feasibility, appraisal and negotiation, the project went on site in January 1996 and was completed in the following January. Through an ERDF grant, the project gained a business advice function and will assist the business development of film and video companies in East London and the Lea Valley. Following a National Lottery award, the premises were opened in September 1997. The workspace element of the project is fully let, despite rents being high for the area. As a whole, the building was named 'The Lux'.

ENO Works

In 1995, DCP became aware of another cultural institution looking for premises, this time through the route of an enterprising planning officer with an interest in opera. The English National Opera needed a new home for its Contemporary Opera Studio and the Baylis Programme (its community involvement project). Their needs were matched up with local property, and a reasonable match was made with the soon to be redundant Shoreditch Library. Helped along with grant funding, the two projects moved into the upper parts of the vacated library in March 1996. Subsequently, ENO agreed a lease on the whole building and, renamed ENO Works, the building provides work space for the aforesaid projects and rehearsal space for its orchestra (and the Covent Garden orchestra, in due course). This was perhaps the least 'economic' of the projects comprising the cultural quarter. It created only a couple of new jobs and was not designed as attraction for visitors, although the temporary visits of the orchestra will presumably have some positive impact on the local economy. Moreover, to accommodate ENO, the library had to be vacated earlier than expected, leaving a 12 month gap between it closing and the opening of its replacement on the Shoreditch Campus (see below). However, these factors were mitigated by the prestige of having a national institution located in Hoxton and by ensuring that the Library received sympathetic new owners, and thus not fall into dereliction. The community programme aspects involve work with schools in Hackney

Cultural quarter and regeneration

Thus alongside the national centre for new circus, the London Centre for film and video, ENO Works added a further cultural centre. Together with the Glasshouse studios and the Blue Note, a genuine cultural quarter was emerging that, on adjacent sites, included two venues, a cinema, a wide range of work space, a number of significant arts and cultural institutions, recording studios, rehearsal space and three cafes/bars. The area was home to cultural production in fields of music, film and video and visual arts, and was a centre for performing arts.

The full potential of the area will not be known until 'The Lux' is fully open and Circus Space's final phase is complete. However, it is clear that a remarkable conjunction of activities is underway which will mark out Hoxton as a unique site of cultural production. It is evident from this outline history that contingency played a big role in the process. The regeneration programme, the granting of Objective 2 status for parts of London, including Hoxton/ Shoreditch and the introduction of National Lottery funding has shaped and aided the process.

However, without the initial designation by the council and by DCP of an arts and cultural focus for the area, it is difficult to see how this series of events would have happened, and the part-accident, part design history has lent the process vitality. It has involved private companies, developers, institutions and not-for-profit bodies in a (mostly) creative interaction. The pursuit of grant funding whenever it was available does not seem to have corrupted the intent of the main players, as can sometimes happen, whilst the need to provide practical implementation plans and to produce economic development outputs helped to introduce pragmatism in regard to implementation.

However, the creation of the cultural quarter has not been without controversy in the local business and residential communities, and a number of questions remain to be addressed. These focus on two areas:

Firstly, what benefits has the local community gained from this activity? Has this fed through to local employment? What impact has this programme had on the self image of the area?

Secondly, is a concentration on cultural industries the best way to stimulate economic development activity in a City Fringe area? What has been the effect on business formation and inward investment? What has been the effect on existing businesses?

Whilst data on these points is likely to be somewhat subjective at this stage, it is worth reviewing the arguments surrounding these issues. As I have indicated, the definition of 'cultural' is critical to this debate. The regeneration initiative has been driven by economic development needs, emphasising those industries related to cultural production, with important subsidiary initiatives relating to tourism. But the community response has been broader than this.

The community response

The key responses (as perceived) are summarised below, which have in turn impacted on the cultural agenda:

Historical neglect

As noted above, Shoreditch was a separate Metropolitan Borough up to 1962, which still had the elements of a distinct economy around manufacturing. Many local residents consider that the incorporation of Shoreditch into Hackney has led to a long period of neglect, especially in relation to council housing and maintenance. The historical changes in the labour market have led to a mismatch of skills to employment and thus to persistent unemployment. One perception is that the regeneration process has not yet led to an increase in obvious employment, with many of the jobs in the arts and cultural industries requiring higher educational attainments not held by local unemployed people.

Social exclusion

The boundary of the City Challenge programme, which has facilitated most of the developments outlined above was drawn between the residential communities and the main development sites and business areas to the west and south. This led to an obvious grievance in relation to the expenditure of urban regeneration monies. The social exclusion is very evident: areas of high unemployment concentrated on council estates, can be graphically illustrated through the comparison of 'prestige' projects versus the run down condition of local estates. Many of the small businesses who 'pioneered' live and work uses in the area in the late 1980's also felt excluded by the assistance given to 'outside' agencies, perhaps forgetting that every community was an outsider once.

Community identity

This sense of social and economic exclusion has been exacerbated by the changes in the local economy. One obvious fact of working in Shoreditch is the evident lack of any joint 'ownership' of the area by local businesses and communities. The clear identity of the area created by its manufacturing past has gone, and has not been replaced by any shared vision. The City support economy could be located anywhere around the City, and hence has few local roots. The cultural economy is not necessarily is this position, and as argued below, can play a key role in defining an area, and giving it kudos. However, it can equally be seen as an imposition on the area and perhaps as a challenge to its traditional identity.

The moral agenda

A further facet of the debate over Shoreditch has been the entry of the Church into the debate over the moral content of regeneration process. The shadow of Canary Wharf hangs metaphorically, as well as literally, over East London, with its symbol of dramatic transformation taking place over the heads of the local population. This concern that local communities should be involved in regeneration work has been added to the moral concerns related to unemployment, youth culture, crime and drugs. Early on the excitement created by the Hoxton developments led to the area being described as a 'new Soho'. This was meant favourably by those who used the expression, meaning the conjugation of media industries and fashionable night time economy that characterised the new Soho. However, in the eyes of the older residents of Hoxton, Soho meant sleaze. Shoreditch had had a marginal sex industry for a long time. The regeneration programme had no ambition to focus on the evening economy, and concentrated on mainstream economic activity, including the cultural industries. However, some community representatives, wilfully or not, took it as read that undesirable evening economy activities were wrapped up in the economic changes to the area. As we shall see below, this was a very partial view of the economic changes to the area.

Licensing and regulation

This concern took a practical form in a number of battles over regulation. The chief target was the Blue Note, on Hoxton Square, which became hugely fashionable as a clubbing location from 1995 onwards. However, due to Hoxton Square's designation as an employment zone, but close to the residential area, this raised a number of questions as to the nature of change in the district. Some of these problems were the club's fault, in terms of early poor management and inadequate investment in sound proofing, but in other ways the club seemed to be a hook on which to hang local concerns about crime and drug culture. These national issues were given local prominence by the club, even though specific complaints seemed hard to come by. Following this, a number of regulatory issues arose around late opening of various restaurants/bars in the area. These tended to be in the south, which might be surprising given the lack of residents in this area and its overall planning designation. However, by this time, a local campaign had grown up around 'the night time economy', which was provoked by Hackney's Council's consultancy study in the Shoreditch area. The council had attempted to follow the lead of cities such as Leeds in formulating ways in which to encourage the evening economy, such as marketing various parts of the borough to evening visitors, consideration of its policies towards licensing and use of pavements for cafes and so on.

Property Prices

One of the more obvious changes to the area over the past two years has been the increase in property prices. As noted above, the last recession led to a slump in values, and hence open to lower rent uses. The increased fashionability of Hoxton has led to an increase in studio rents and the inward move of more mainstream businesses. These include those 'cultural industries' that feed off the City market, such as graphic designers, as well as film and video production companies and music businesses. Much of the rise in prices has been driven by mixed developments, involving live/work accommodation or straightforward residential uses. This process has not been seen as benefiting local people , who cannot afford the prices of the private housing (which hence goes to 'outsiders'). The cost of studio space has escalated, and existing arts and crafts businesses feel they are being priced out of the area. Ironically, their effect in making the area fashionable may been too successful for their own good. The unauthorised use of studios as living space (as part of the 'lifestyle' nature of these business) has encouraged the onset of live and work developments (taking their cue from similar and successful developments in neighbouring Clerkenwell), which have in turn encouraged purely residential developments. It is not yet clear whether all new permissions will be granted. Nonetheless, the effect has been to create a speculative market driven mainly by residential possibilities. The *Sunday Times* (3 August 1997) reported properties in Hoxton Square being marketed for over £300,000 per floor.

Hence community concerns present a complex mixture of historical, social, economic, political and moral issues. The net result has been a community campaign that has articulately opposed the change occurring in the area.

Culture and regeneration

The quotation below may help to further illustrate the culture/regeneration debate. It is a satirical piece from *D Tour*, the local listings magazine:

> Another new comer to Hoxton is Lytton St. John, or Nobby as he prefers to be called. With his carefully crumpled Kenzo fatigues and expertly tailored dreadlocks, Nobby says he was attracted to the area by

Hoxton Square. Photograph © David Gibson

> cheap studio space - 'a big studio flat only costs about £90,000' - and the sense of regeneration here...How would he define the character of Hoxton? 'One long party' grins Nobby, a man with no discernible income, but generous relatives.
>
> As we walk back to his apartment, Nobby discusses New York, Brit - pop and his girlfriend's job as a researcher on the 'Girlie Show'. Stepping past an ageing drunk on the corner of Hoxton Square, Nobby comments, 'Why don't these people just get up and do something! I mean, open up a cyber cafe, set up a gallery, write a Channel Four proposal or something....'
>
> Before I leave this atmospheric location, the buzz of rising prices overlaid by the faint smell of ground coffee, I run into a grungy youth being sick. An artist, perhaps? Tony is in fact unemployed. 'I used to live round here but the landlord put the rent up, renovated the place, sold it to a graphic designer or something'. Still, he must find the cultural renewal here marvellous surely. 'Er, not really, I'm still signing on. Be all right if I was an interior designer, I suppose'. (Nick Houghton, *D Tour*, June 1997).

Satire aside, this article touches on some real issues. The possibility of 'regenerating' an area, whilst not improving life for the people who live there (or making their plight worse) is a worrying one. It does not take too much imagination to think of areas of London like Notting Hill or Clerkenwell, where fashionable areas exist cheek by jowl with significant deprivation. If urban regeneration only results in new 'Trustafarian' havens, clearly it will have failed, even if the net result is an increase in cultural activity and venues.

It is worth mentioning at this point the way that Government policy in regard to urban regeneration practise has influenced this debate. City Challenge was the first regeneration regime that took a competitive approach to obtaining Government resources. At the same time, it raised the profile of the partnership agenda, which influenced the creation of autonomous organisations or agencies. This is not the place to discuss all the ramifications of this, but the tension between partnership (with the consultation process that automatically comes with this) and delivering regeneration outputs, expenditure and 'leverage' (especially private investment) is worth noting, especially in the 'top-down' culture that dominated the previous government's approach to regeneration issues. Even leaving this point aside, it is fair to point out that a regeneration programme can get lost in consultation and deliver nothing, and thereby lose its funding and credibility, or it can successfully deliver its programme, but at the expense of local participation and input. One factor of importance here was the need to demonstrate success in economic development and job creation. This meant that job creation and business development had to be sought in growth sectors, which pre-eminently included the cultural industries in the early 1990s.

A further point relates to the movement of the property market. As noted above, the early 1990s created low rents in the area due to the recession in financial services and an over provision in office space. However, with the economy on the move again, this situation was temporary. This is little to do with the regeneration process, although it does raise the issues around mixed development. However, in conventional economic development terms, the increase in demand for property is usually seen as a sign of rising prosperity. As noted above, the council had fought a losing battle to retain the traditional industrial uses in the area, and following the enforced change of policy in the 1980s, it was inevitable that moves in the market would begin to influence the area. The City Challenge programme had funded a small number of minor live/work developments though its small business grant programme, but the major proposals had not received support, as there was continuing concern at how live/work and residential developments would have the potential to drive out existing employment.

These points are made to underline the limited options that are sometimes available in implementing urban regeneration policies. However, this is not to concede that the support of the cultural economy in Hoxton has been without value, far from it.

Catalytic effects

This positive point of view would include the following points.

- the transformation of long-standing dereliction into a vibrant area
- the attraction of investment to the area
- the creation of employment, not just in the areas of core cultural production but in the ancillary areas of entertainment and tourism.
- the creation of linkages with the wider economy
- the opportunity to modernise the area and make it competitive in terms of attracting investment.

All the components of the cultural quarter have, or will have, the effect of creating new economic activity, and even leaving aside the secondary effect of visitors' expenditure, the creation of the cultural quarter has created over 250 jobs, perhaps half of these new, with the remainder existing jobs new to the area. A largely derelict and decaying area has been transformed into a thriving place of work and a growing visitor attraction.

Moreover, the creation of the cultural quarter has provided a stimulus to the wider regeneration process, and the combination of cultural production and economic development runs through a number or regeneration activities close by, which have fed off each other to an extent. These include:

- the development of last vacant council-owned site in the vicinity, on the south side of the Hoxton Market and fronting Old Street, for a 220 bed hotel, planned to be complete by July 1998 and employing around 70 people;
- the creation of Metro New Media (part of London Guildhall University), a training, educational, R & D and business start up space, established in pilot form on Old Street, but planned for a much larger location, on Hackney Community College's Shoreditch Campus;
- the inclusion of the Geffrye Design Centre, a marketing and exhibition centre for furniture designer/makers and interior designers in the major new gallery being built by the Geffrye Museum (the national museum for domestic interiors, located in Hoxton);
- the creation of the Hoxton Bibliotech, a voluntary sector training project covering publishing, new media and journalism, based around an arts/listing magazine, *D Tour*, which covers the north and east London area.
- the establishment of a world music centre and other media-related education and training on the new Shoreditch Campus;

Hence the setting of a cultural and arts agenda as part of the regeneration process should be seen as highly successful. Apart from achieving results in its own right, the cultural activity created at Hoxton Square appears to have influenced and aided neighbouring regeneration schemes and affected the decision of mainstream businesses such as the franchisees who are developing the Old Street Holiday Inn.

Economic impact

Before moving on to specifics on this point, I want to address the issue of what cultural industries are. These groups of businesses are difficult to define in terms of SIC (Standard Industrial Classification) definitions, and connect with each other in ways that are not always obvious. In Hackney, the vast City fringe economy further distorts this picture, with a number of 'cultural' businesses (printing and publishing, graphic design, advertising and some photographers), serving the City market, and having little to do with the markets associated with cultural production *per se* (e.g. music production or film and video production.)

I think it is best to think of these industries as focusing on cultural production in its own right: on music, visual arts, performing arts and film and video. Multi-media is also part of this set of industries to the extent that it has formed a new medium by joining existing media together through digital technology. However, to the extent that it is about expanding means of communications (i.e. through the Internet), it is a business service. Hence a consideration of the economic impact of the cultural field needs to consider both cultural production, and the wider economy, including tourism and business services.

Visual Media

The first point here is that visual media industries do not have to be located anywhere in particular. They are traditionally associated in London with Soho, but in recent times have moved further west into Kensington and Hammersmith. Outside London, several cities have had initiatives to associate themselves with these industries, notably Manchester and Sheffield. The development of on-line and digital capability means that cultural production that employs this technology can be sited more or less anywhere. For instance some Soho-based film houses are bidding for the Hollywood market as film rushes can be transferred on line rather than requiring courier delivery. Hence any area can try for this market, but has to face considerable competition. However East London can offer proximity to the City market, which is attractive for some elements of the industry, whilst rents are lower than the West End. In Shoreditch, warehouse conversions are attractive and suitable for studio/office uses. Harder to define, but as important, is the sense of the East End as a culturally interesting and creative area. The concentration of visual artists, including a number of famous names helps this (e.g. Gilbert and George and Rachel Whiteread) whilst East London is also regarded as a source of talent for the music industry. The development of Hoxton has attracted media businesses to move into the area, including music, film and video and multi-media businesses. It is too early to judge how strong a trend this is, but it appears that the success of the cultural quarter has made the area acceptable as a location for existing businesses in these sectors. Performing arts have certainly benefited from the creation of new venues at Circus Space and elsewhere. The visual arts have benefited from the number of new galleries that have opened and the provision of refurbished studio space.

Tourism

In relation to tourism, the most evident beneficiary has been the entertainment and catering sector. This serves two markets in Shoreditch. Firstly local businesses, who find good quality bars/restaurants a useful facility. The increased number of media businesses has made the area more attractive for catering businesses, and a number of new restaurants and cafe/bars have opened up, in addition to those located around Hoxton Square itself. Secondly, there is a growing visitor market. In addition to the new attractions in Hoxton Square, there is the Comedy Cafe, which is planning to expand and the Brick Lane Music Hall (since September 1996 located in Curtain Road). The Holiday Inn hotel will attract approximately 17,000 visitors a year once it is opened. Since the Holiday Inn's market is budget tourism, this is likely to stimulate more catering/entertainment enterprises to locate close to it.

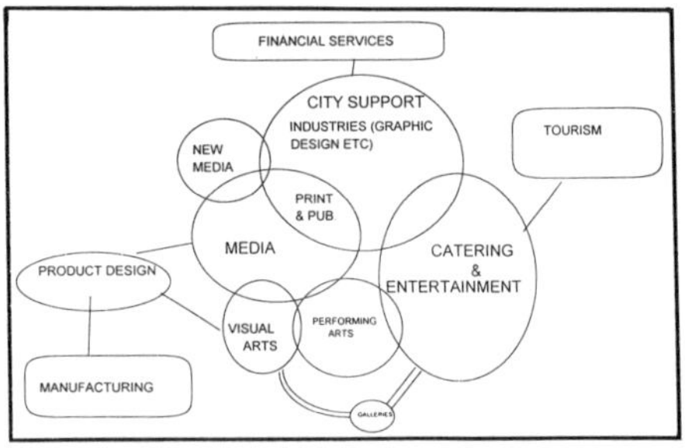

Links with other sectors

This diagram is designed to show how intimately the nest of related cultural industries are involved with other sectors of the economy. It is not a long step from considering cultural industries as an adjunct to tourism, part of the conglomeration of sectors servicing the City's financial institutions or part of the design industry contributing to manufacturing. One of the underdeveloped linkages that exists is between the craft and design industry and product development for manufacturing. These range from designer-makers, usually sole traders, chasing commissions or producing small batches of products to design-based companies, manufacturing elsewhere. They represent a link between the older Shoreditch manufacturing economy and the arts economy, and represent an important part of the live/work economy. An example of this is the wide range of fashion designers that work in Hackney. This area is a further instance of the adaptability of businesses working in the arts, design and media areas. However, the main economy of the area, financial, business and professional services, dominates the economic output of the area, and provides 55 per cent of its employment, compared with the 7 per cent working in the cultural industries. 35 per cent of the entire employment in the London Borough of Hackney as a whole is located in its City fringe wards. (This is not the same as local people employed, of course.) It could be argued that the cultural economy is an irrelevance, as location to the City market, and its exploitation, dominates the economic calculations of businesses in these sectors. Some of the activities related to the cultural economy and related areas of tourism and entertainment might be seen as actively repellent to its business needs, for instance through the hogging of scarce car parking space, or bringing visitors to the area that do not relate to the City support market.

However, there are strong counter arguments to this. Firstly, as noted above, there is significant overlap between the fields of cultural production and many of the business and operational services, for example, graphic design, advertising, photography, communications (including new media) and printing and publishing. There is no doubt that this group of businesses benefit from the creativity and cachet of working in a 'creative' and fashionable area. This is indicated by the number of graphic design industries that have recently colonised Charlotte Road, south of Old Street. It is manifested in a concrete way by the need of these businesses to congregate together for joint working, sourcing staff and making business contacts. Secondly, the improvement of facilities in the hotel and entertainment sectors will benefit the area in terms of entertaining and housing business clients or attracting staff. Given the increasing competition that the City of London faces in terms of maintaining its position as a world leader in the financial services, it seems reasonable to maintain that it needs to develop areas such as Shoreditch and Hoxton to ensure that good quality ancillary businesses continue to be located nearby, and that visitor attractions exist to cater for employees located there, or for business visitors. In this context, the cultural economy has a vital part to play.

A tougher proposition is that the growth in financial services might drive out the weaker sections of the cultural economy. A graphic example of this is the demolition of the neighbouring Spitalfields Market, in Tower Hamlets, for the new LIFFE Exchange. Since the removal of the fruit and vegetable market to Leyton, the market has become home to a flourishing group of cultural industries, most of whom will need new homes upon demolition. Whilst Hoxton is not faced with such a development, the increase in property values threatens a more insidious displacement of arts businesses. As stated above, this has little to do with the regeneration process, but is a factor to be taken into account when drawing up regeneration policies. Is it best to treat this as an inevitability, and concentrate on accessing the new jobs created for local people, or should this process be fought? However, this proposition is perhaps too stark. Whilst the growth in financial, business and professional services, and its effect on the local community is likely to be the headline story in the City Fringe in the near future, areas like Shoreditch and Hoxton are likely to continue to provide a mixed range of employment. As I discussed above, parts of the cultural industries are embedded in the City support economy in any case, and the Hoxton Square developments will act as a magnet for attracting media and cultural industries. My feeling is that the growth of the City will have not have a major effect on Hoxton, and although weaker sectors may be driven out, the arts/cultural and tourism business sectors as a whole are too well entrenched to be easily dislodged at this stage. A more problematic issue is the growth of the area as a fashionable residential base, which has the potential to drive out existing employment of all sorts, whilst not providing any affordable accommodation for local people.

Overview

A good economic case can be made for the development of the cultural quarter in the sense of the development of economic activity in the core areas of cultural production, the development of the related sectors of tourism, entertainment and catering, and in its connection with other sectors. Whilst many of the jobs associated with the former area may require specialised levels of skills and education beyond the reach of many local residents, the jobs in the ancillary industries should be within the reach of a wider group of people. Ironically, these latter industries include those most opposed by local pressure groups, and clearly there needs to be an open discussion on how far the club/ restaurant sector is allowed to develop. It would seem reasonable to support its development in designated employment areas, but clearly to oppose it where it causes disturbance to residential areas. No one would mourn the disappearance of the 'red light' economy on Shoreditch High Street and neighbouring Commercial Street.

A local employment policy backed up by appropriate training is essential, and indeed such a policy is in place in relation to the Holiday Inn hotel. Overall, tourism is regarded as a growth industry, along with many sectors of the cultural industries, such as film and video, music and multi-media. Apart from this obvious benefit, these sectors have the advantage of being attractive to young people in terms of training and employment. There is already substantial provision of training and education in place in relation to the cultural industries, and there is scope for enhancement in terms of quantity and quality.

Another point is how the development of the cultural industries will effect the future identity of the area. As stated earlier, this is a moot point at present. However there is evidence that some local residents and businesses are adopting a more positive approach to the regeneration process, and are starting to express themselves through the Shoreditch Development Campaign. As noted above, Shoreditch and Hoxton are historically important in the production and performance of art and popular culture and there is no reason why the historic background of the area should not engage with the new arrivals to produce a new identity. This may lead to bizarre thoughts of music hall drum & bass or cockney opera, but hopefully the sense of this may survive such imaginings. The important thing is to create forums for such an identity to evolve. One of Hackney's strengths is its co-existence of different cultures, and the Hoxton Square development should allow this to develop one step further, given time and good will. Programmes such as ENO's Baylis Programme, taking opera to schools and old people's homes, may help this.

A more serious step is the development of regeneration programmes that target the residential communities of Hoxton, especially in the fields of housing, community facilities, training and employment. The East London URBAN programme has started work on these points as has the City Fringe Partnership, an SRB-funded programme concentrating on the historic quarters of Shoreditch, Spitalfields and Clerkenwell. This has a 'Pathways to Employment' element already, although whilst there is much more work to be done here, this approach will build on the substantial investment made through City Challenge in education and training infrastructure and programming. Further programmes contributing to the community economic development of the area will include the European Objective 2 Priority 4 programme and possibly Labour's New Deal.

The challenge for local businesses may not be in protecting low rents, which would seem to be a lost cause in all but not-for-profit ghettos, but to encourage the stronger companies to become more competitive. This would involve the encouragement of specialised (and high value-added) tourism, the development of City markets, the development of marketing using new media, the development of business sectors using digital technology and new media and the forging of links between design and manufacturing. This is a diverse programme, but one that fully reflects the diversity of the business sectors considered here. The growth of digitalisation, incidentally, with its convergence of text, sound and video production with computing and communications technologies, is a fair approximation of the growth in the need for flexibility and multi-skilling that many of the cultural industry businesses can offer. In Shoreditch you can find the most modern of industries working alongside the most ancient. For instance, I can think of a computing company producing CD-Roms for the British Library that is a stone's throw from a paper-maker restoring documents for the same organisation. This sort of diversity may yet prove a strength rather than a weakness.

Conclusion

I have outlined how the urban regeneration agenda has been effective in creating a cultural quarter around Hoxton Square. I have also indicated how this process has been received in the local residential and business communities. I have investigated what effect this process has had on the local and wider economy.

Earlier in this article I asked two questions as to whether this process has had a beneficial impact on the local community, and what value the cultural industries have in the wider economic development of the area. In relation to the first point, I have pointed to the seriousness of many community concerns. However, I have also tried to show that many of these concerns are mis-addressed, and derive from the complex of concerns around unemployment, crime, poverty, social exclusion and perceived moral decline, rather than the economic development entailed in establishing the cultural quarter. I have argued that the Hoxton developments have provided a vital stimulus to the development of the area, which would most likely have remained largely derelict without the creativity and energy of the organisations that have moved into the area.

Similar points relate to the second question. The set of arts, craft, design and media industries, referred to in shorthand as the 'cultural industries' provide a relatively small part of the employment of the area. Yet, any local economy that fails to include a component from these industries risks not being competitive, as the skills they offer are essential for the competitiveness of a range of other industries, ranging from the City Support industries, to tourism or manufacturing. The challenge in

Hoxton and Shoreditch is to ensure that local benefits accrue from the cultural quarter and its related industries, and that an inclusive process of community development takes place.

The wider challenge might be stated as the reconnection of the economic development agenda with the regeneration agenda. The Hoxton cultural quarter is a good example of the range of responses and factors that regeneration activity can involve. I would argue that a dynamic must be created between these two agendas. Economic development is essential to improve deprived areas, but without a consideration of wider issues, such as the history of an area or the standard of its housing and facilities, it risks being irrelevant to local people. However, a purely community development approach to regeneration has risks of a greater sort, those associated with raising unrealistic hopes or failing to connect with the wider labour market and economy. This latter option may be easier in some ways, by meeting immediate community demands, but may fail to attain the long term development of a deprived area. The regeneration process in Hoxton and Shoreditch has been a good example of how these agendas have interacted, and as such it is a good place to start from in continuing this debate.

Thanks to D Tour *Magazine for allowing me to quote from the Nick Houghton piece and to John Burrow at DCP for invaluable information on Shoreditch's planning background.*

'Welcome to the East'

The opening of the East London Museum of Science and Art

Cathy Ross

The East London Museum of Science and Art, otherwise known as the Bethnal Green branch of the South Kensington Museum, is one of London's more under-discussed Victorian institutions.[1] As a cultural initiative for East London it has been overshadowed by its later neighbours, the People's Palace opened in 1887 and the Toynbee Hall art exhibitions culminating in the opening of the Whitechapel Art Gallery in 1901. As a museum it has been overshadowed by its more well-connected parent in West London. Social and cultural historians have generally passed over the Bethnal Green Museum, and this despite the fact that as an institution wholly run by a department of national government it was a uniquely early example of direct state intervention into the life of the East.

Despite this neglect, it is nevertheless arguable that the East London Museum was one of the Victorian metropolis's most significant cultural institutions; the combination of what it was, where it was located and who was running it making it something of a lightning conductor for ideas from every point of the historiographical compass. Bethnal Green touches on many points of debate: the function of national government in relation to local endeavour; the acceptance of education as a legitimate interest of national government; the role of objects and 'object lessons' in Victorian systems of knowledge; state responsibility towards 'the labouring classes'; the transmission of cultural ideas; the nature of the difference between West and East London; the development of the twin notions of national museums and national cultural property.

It is also possible to argue that the opening of the museum in June 1872 by the Prince and Princess of Wales was one of East London's must significant events. 'Welcome to the East' was the wording on one of the banners displayed along the route of the royal procession, reflecting the fact that this was the first State visit to the East End within living memory. As such the event was significant in itself, but in the context of the 1870s the event was imbued with even deeper resonances. The day was a ceremonial expression of the country's new political mood and, in its own small way, the East London Museum was as much a symbol of the realignment of the State, following the suffrage reform of 1867, as the Education Act of 1870. This meaning can not have been lost on the East Londoners, to whom the unprecedented sight of a member of the Royal Family in the Bethnal Green Road must have been as strong a signifier of change as the new Board Schools erupting into the landscape.

In this short article I will look at the opening of this unlikely but revealing national museum.[2] It should be said at the start that looking just at the opening does not do justice to the Bethnal Green Museum as a whole, since the story of its accident-prone operation by the Science and Art Department in the first 25 years of its life is one of the most interesting things about it. Over that period the 'brilliant success' of 1872 was transformed into the 'rubbish heap' of the 1898 Select Committee on the Museums of the Science and Art Department, whose members, including both John Burns and Bethnal Green's Conservative MP Sir Mancherjee Bhownaggree,

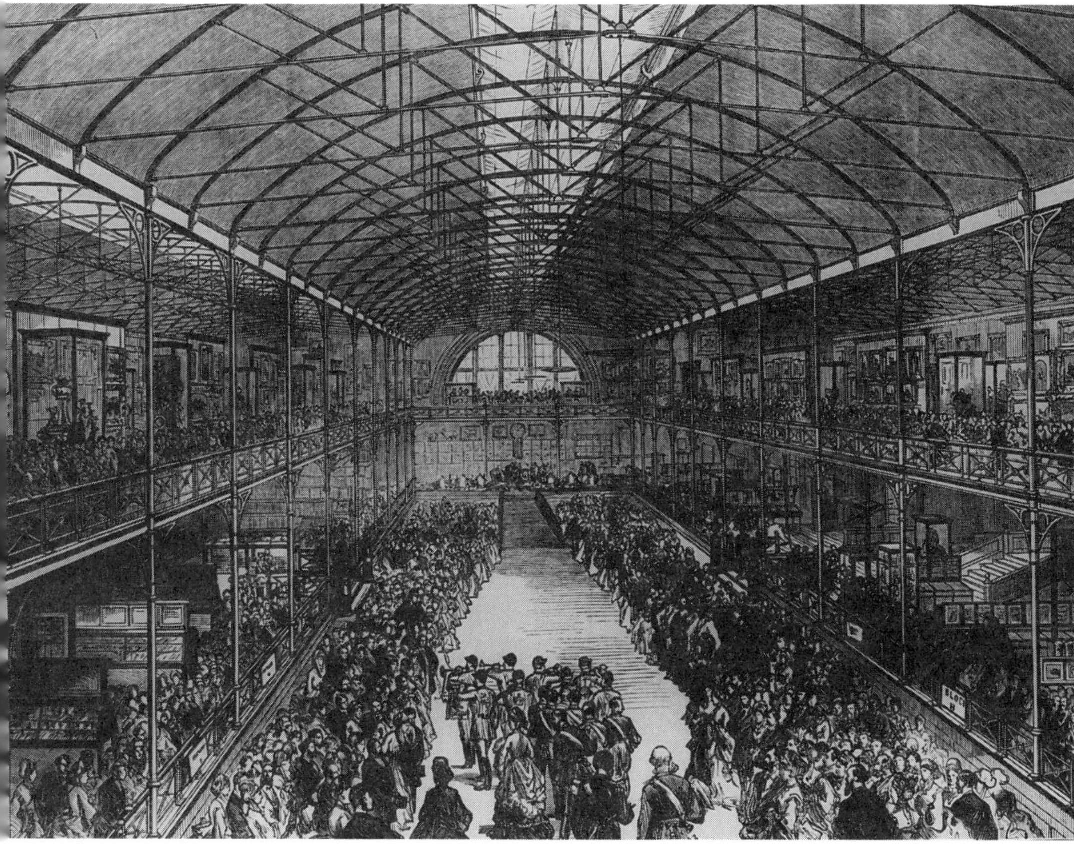

The opening ceremony: woodcut from The Illustrated London News, *29 June 1872. © Tower Hamlets Local History Library*

united in the conclusion that the museum had been a disgraceful waste of public money and an insult to the people of the East End. During that time a bizarre selection of material culture had been laid before the Bethnal Green public, ranging from objects whose national 'value' was undisputed, such as the collection of National Portraits, to curiosities such as a 700 feet long rope made from Japanese hair which was said to have used up the female hair of an entire province. Looking just at the opening, then, we see the East London Museum of Science and Art at its finest hour, as a pristine initiative, its logic and justifications untested by practical application and un-sabotaged by objects, visitors or officials.

This opening is, however, interesting in itself and what this article seeks to do is to explore some of the ideas that surround the event in terms of what they say about the 'Eastness' of East London at the time. What did the day mean in terms of the relationship between East and West London? Did a day designed to symbolise the coming together of East and West in harmony for the national good in fact express the opposite? How was the cultural identity of this part of the metropolis perceived, expressed and indeed contested through the press reports of the grand events in Bethnal Green on midsummer's day 1872?

And the events were indeed grand. The sun shone. There was a procession with military bands, an escort of Life Guards, horses and open carriages carrying grooms, equerries, Ladies of the Bed Chamber, bishops, peers and the Lord Mayor of London. The Prince of Wales was dressed in the red uniform of a general officer, the Princess 'in a pink bonnet and polonaise of the same colour, trimmed with point lace over a crimson petticoat'. Exotic touches were added by the presence of a North American Indian chief in a ceremonial embroidered blanket suit and a party from the Burmese embassy in white robes and gold vestments. Bethnal Green rose to the occasion with the route of the procession 'black with human ants', and 'planted thick with curious sightseers': the men in 'shirt sleeves and a long tobacco pipe ......while the fairer sex was clad almost universally in cotton print frocks'. The cheering was deafening and the route was heavily decorated with flags, banners and home-made decorations 'of a more primitive character'. Deference and loyalty were both much in evidence on the banners according to what was reported: 'Thank you for your kind visit' 'Long live Royalty, Science and Art', 'God bless the Prince and his Physician' and 'Welcome to the East.'

Looking at this one event with the ideas of West and East London in mind is an interesting exercise for several reasons. Firstly, much of the comment about the new museum was conceptualised in terms of west and east, a notion strengthened by the convenient fact that the museum's parent, the South Kensington Museum, was located in the West. The notion of the separate identities of West and East London with the new museum acting as a bridge between the two across which the West could travel, pervaded everything. Here, for example, is a comment on Sir Richard Wallace, whose collection of art treasures provided the museum with its opening loan exhibition: 'Sir Richard Wallace has chosen the East-End for the exhibition simply on the grounds that he believes the poor of the neighbourhood will be not only pleased with the exhibition itself, but benefited by the influx of the rich from the West-End and other parts into their district'.

I know him by the pictures

The second point is simply that this was an extraordinary occasion. The conjunction of West and East through the arrival of the State in full splendour in 'one of the poorest and dingiest quarters of London' was both encounter and collision, an occasion of contrasts that seem no less striking now than they must have in the 1870s. The West brought to the East a public display of the private property of Sir Richard Wallace: objects of fabulous value such as Sevres porcelain, gilt bronze candelabra, works by Rembrandt and Leonardo. In return the East welcomed its visitors from the West with a public display of their own household property:

> ...the householders simply stripped their rooms of the most showy objects they contained and stuck them up outside. Old rugs, carpets, curtains, tea trays, chimney-piece ornaments and fireplace finery in tissue paper were all included in this frank and homely system of embellishment. Here and there a shopkeeper had come out strong with crimson-cloth and Dutch-metal; but the most significant and touching feature of the scene was the sincerity with which the people produced their simple, domestic contribution to the general display. It was in every sense a genuine popular festival.

No less dramatic was the encounter between the people themselves, as the West stared at the East staring at the West:

> It was curious to observe the astonished gaze with which many of these people looked at the Life Guards and at Royalty. The constant exclamation 'That's him, I know him by the pictures!' told the listener that thousands of the people of the metropolis had never seen the Prince before; and from their exclamations of admiration in respect of the Household troops, 'Ain't they fine' and 'Ain't they beautiful', it was pretty clear that a field officer's escort of Life Guards was a scene which Bethnal Green had not witnessed within the memory of the oldest inhabitant.

The exclamations of the Prince and Princess were not recorded although it was certainly suggested that the feeling of astonishment was mutual.

> Until their visit to Bethnal Green they could scarcely have known much about that astonishing province in the empire of London, which is tenanted by an even more astonishing population, whose manners, customs, garbs and facial appearance seem to differ from those of the neighbours of north, south, east and west, as widely and as irreconcilably as Brittany differs from Bloomsbury.

All this is predictable. Many of the press accounts of the opening are riddled with metaphors of foreign travel and exploration, Bethnal Green being seen as 'terra incognita', a strange land of 'metropolitan orientals'. So can the opening do any more than merely underscore the presence of the fault line between West and East in the Victorian metropolis? In the very broad sense, no, but what the detail of this particular occasion does provide is some reflections on the subtleties of the 'difference' that divided the two quarters, a difference that was rather more complex than a simple scheme of 'us and them', excluded or included according to class, culture or ownership of property. In addition it offers an insight into the national psyche at a point when the debate about the place of the working classes in the nation was at a particularly intense point. The events of the day were extraordinary and they occurred at a time when established social hierarchies were being if not reworked then at least questioned: were the workers the nation's new 'masters';[3] was the difference between East and West one of opposition, ranking or complement? The opening of the museum provided an opportunity for the born-again nation to reflect on all of this, and it is perhaps no surprise that this reflection can seem almost schizophrenic in its mixture of fervent self-congratulation and deep unease.

The most seductive strand in the post-Reform Act mood, and one which certainly dominates the accounts of this particularly event, was the belief that here was a nation in perfect harmony. The fact of the museum was taken as evidence of the happy truth that although differences existed between West and East, the two quarters were perfectly matched, like pieces in a jigsaw, both enjoying the notional equality which nationhood bestowed on all sorts and conditions of men, irrespective of their obvious inequalities in life. The embodiment of this was, of course, the figure of the Prince and the rapturous reception, 'difficult to exaggerate', given to him by Bethnal Green was universally remarked on, as was the political meaning of the people's enthusiasm. 'It is to be hoped', said the *Times,* 'that it was witnessed by the handful of English Republicans who feel it in their duty to enter a protest against Royalty. If it was they must in their hearts feel that they have no followers among the masses of the English working classes'.

If Prince bound people together in nationhood, so did the new museum which was presented almost in terms of political economy, as a perfect fit between the East's scarcity and the West's surplus. As indeed was the case with the fabric of the building. The museum was housed in the re-erected 'Brompton boilers' the temporary structure put up in the late 1850s to house the Museum of

Practical Art, the nucleus of the museum complex at South Kensington, and now made redundant by Henry Cole's extravagant new building programme. More interestingly, the 'substantial iron railings' which surrounded the Bethnal Green building were 'transferred from Hyde Park, where (they were) no longer wanted'. These are said to be the railings pulled down in the great suffrage demonstration of 1866.[4] If this is so, their presence around the plot of government-owned land in East London, formerly part of the common ground of Bethnal Green, was a powerful symbol which could be read in a number of ways.

Not at all

The content of the new museum was undoubtedly informed by the West's surplus as much as the East's needs. Thanks to the presence of the Wallace Collection, the museum's inaugural temporary exhibition, much was made of the refining and elevating influence of Art. However, the collections that the Science and Art Department had decided to transfer to the East were not Art at all. What were dispatched to Bethnal Green were the Food and Animal Products Collections, put together for the Great Exhibition as part of Prince Albert's grand 'animal/ vegetable /mineral' typology, and not seen in public since. This brought some strange and curious things to Bethnal Green: Dikka bread from West Africa, shark's fins and sea slugs from the Far East, plus 'many interesting diagrams'. The Museum was also given 'an important series of examples of economic entomology', a maverick collection of wax models of insects.[5] The phrase, much proclaimed around the time of the opening, was that Bethnal Green was to house 'objects of science and art, being national property which are insufficiently provided for elsewhere'. The promoters of the museum from the East took this to mean national property of the order of the National Gallery's Turner Bequest, access to which was then a matter of public concern. To the Science and Art Department, however, the phrase meant 'certain collections being national property which occupy space now urgently required for more pressing purposes'.[6] In other words collections which South Kensington no longer wanted.

To return to the question of national harmony and the perfect fit between West and East. How were the East Enders themselves portrayed? Perhaps inevitably many of the papers described for their readers in the West a tribe of docile, deferential and impossibly long suffering beings, whose poverty had somehow left their essential English qualities of good taste and moral rectitude untouched. According to the *Times*, which waxed particularly sentimental

'The visitors round about us were expressing their comments upon these freely enough', an illustration from Cassel's Family Magazine, *1883.*
© Tower Hamlets Local History Library

about the character and conduct of the Bethnal Greeners, 'a better behaved multitude than that which assembled to see and cheer the Prince and Princess yesterday has never been gathered in any portion of the metropolis'. There was no sign of ruffianism but every sign of gratitude for the interest that had been taken in them: 'they are a grateful people'. Accounts of the museum's early visitors made much of the 'inate good taste' of the East Enders and marvelled at the fact that 'the crowd who peered intently on the works of Meissonier might have been a crowd of connoisseurs'.

The Bethnal Green Slander

Did the East Enders recognise themselves in this sentimentalised picture? The interesting point here is that yes, they did. If this picture of the working class was a construction of the West it was one the East collaborated willingly in. At least such is the conclusion one can draw from the immediate aftermath of the opening. In a letter to the *Times* two days later, Septimus Hansard, the vicar of Bethnal Green and one of the Museum's East End promoters, praised their coverage as being written 'in a kindly and truthful spirit', in contrast to the coverage in some other papers. Hansard was voicing a feeling widely shared in Bethnal Green that wrong had been done to the district. The Bethnal Green Slander, as the episode came to be known, provoked a variety of reactions: local 'indignation meetings' were held, during which newspaper accounts of the opening ceremony were read aloud; a boycott of the offending papers was organised; a print was circulated promising summary justice to all those who 'wilfully slander the people of Bethnal Green'.

Hansard was probably the author of a long letter which appeared in *The Echo* on July 6th, under the pseudonym 'One of Them'. This explained the cause of Bethnal Green's grievance: 'we are represented as beings beyond the pale of humanity, unshapely phenomena ... and the aristocratic visitors are, as it were, cautioned against the contamination of us monsters'. According to 'One of Them' the East was presented as a freak show at which the fashionable world might 'stop and laugh, and 'there is something intensely cruel in spurning us away when we come forward with extended hands and grateful hearts; in misrepresenting people who have but indifferent occasions of protesting, and assume their most cheerful look, their best appearance, to receive more worthily their wealthy countryman'.

So what had caused such offence to be taken? The two culprits were *The Daily Telegraph* and *The Daily News*, and in both cases the offence was to concentrate on the inhabitants of the Boundary Street end of Bethnal Green. This notorious patch of poverty was the first part of the East that the visitors from the West saw as they passed beyond the City's boundaries, and the journalists could not resist the temptation to melodramatise. *The Telegraph* had the Prince passing through 'dwarfs and hunchbacks, those creatures bent double, those crooked and bandy and rickety babes... Here yesterday female ugliness of face and form, in black monotonous unvarying typification was predominant. Sickly mothers nursing sickly babies; sickly girls toying in a sickly manner with sickly weaver boys, listless emaciated middle-aged women; dreadful old women as ugly as sin, who looked as though they supported nature on a diet of Lucifer matches and gin'. The *Daily News* described ' gaunt ragged men, stunted narrow-chested, spider-

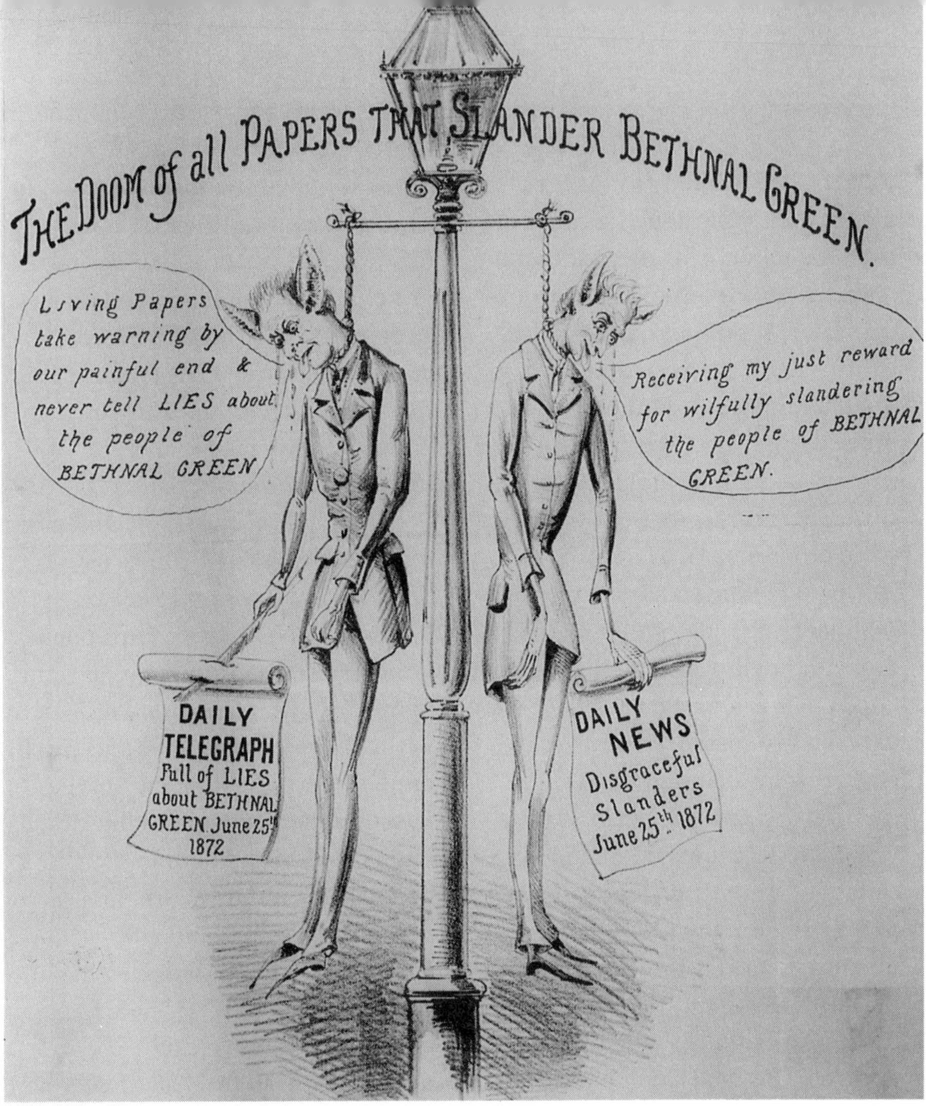

'The Doom of all Papers that Slander Bethnal Green', anonymous lithograph.
© Tower Hamlets Local History Library

limbed, by privation from their mother's breast.... lean, wan-faced women, bareheaded in limp dingy prints, who as they cuddled to their breasts hydrocephalous infants, gazed in a kind of stunted amazement at the novel splendour'.

There are two ways of reading Bethnal Green's grievance at passages like these. One is a sense of wrong being done to the unfortunate Boundary Street people themselves by such brutally frank portrayals. The other, and infinitely more likely, explanation is the sense of wrong being done to the respectable Bethnal Greeners by lumping them in with the Boundary Street people. It was not so much the underlining of the distance between West and East that caused offence, it was the West's failure to recognise the distance between East-respectable, and East-residuum, a distance which should have kept East-respectable safely on the side of the national 'us' rather than the outcast 'them'.

The Bethnal Green Slander appears to have died away in a matter of days, but within a matter of months other causes for disharmony emerged. There was the question of Sunday opening, where W.R. Foster was forced to admit in the House of Commons that the principle of not opening museums on Sunday, long contested on the grounds of access for the working man, had been broken at Bethnal Green by the admission of peers and MPs on special Sunday passes issued by Cole. There was the question of the landscaping of the grounds, which provoked more questions in the House and letters to the *Times*. A more serious broken promise on the Government's part was the failure to erect a School of Science and Art and a library. These had been part of the original scheme; and, at least on the East London side, were understood to be the main justifications for the Science and Art Department's expenditure of public money. Nothing had been done by Spring 1873 when questions in the House, letters to the *Times* and a public meeting in Bethnal Green all called on the government to fulfil its promise but without success. It was no surprise that the 1898 Commission pointed to this as one of the central charges against the Science and Art Department's stewardship of the museum: 'no arrangement having ever been made to provide any sort of technical instruction, the object of the inception of the museum has remained entirely unrealised and justly caused grave discontent in the whole of the East End'.

'A show of public festivity'

It is this failure to erect a School of Science and Art that perhaps points to one fundamental difference between East and West in this particular encounter: the absence of any consensus as to what the museum was for and, by extension, a lack of consensus about the possibilities of social change. To the East the museum was seen as an agent of social change within a dynamic society, quickening the processes that suffrage and educational reform had activated. To the East it was a catalyst in every sphere, particularly economic, and it is no accident that the speeches from the Bethnal Green side at the museum's opening should have connected the institution to the East End's industrial character.

The West, by contrast, could be said to have seen the museum firstly as a symbolic presence and secondly as an agent of social stability, reinforcing what was there already, consolidating the State's ability to manage its existing collections of national property. Despite the rhetoric of State-funded technical education, to which the Science and Art Department clung grimly, however contradictory their actions, the Bethnal Green Museum's only relationship to the economic character of East London was to its past rather than any possible future. The museum was seen as something of a consolation prize, and *The Illustrated London News* report was not untypical when it wrote simply that 'This was a gratifying occasion for the poor people of that rather shabby and depressed quarter. It needs to be cheered now and then with a show of public festivity and with the display of beautiful objects, if nothing can be done for the revival of its industrial prosperity'.

Beneath many of the upbeat accounts of the cheering crowds runs a sense of futility at the evidence of real, endemic poverty that the contrasts of the day pointed up: set against the glittering occasion was 'monotonous meanness and dullness. The whole life of the people seems to be washed down to a dingy, ashen monotone'. Henry James, who visited the museum after its opening took a sceptical, even sour, view of the institution's aspirations and doubted whether even the 'consolatory charm of art' could do anything to help 'the haggard paupers of Bethnal Green'.

Henry Cole recorded the day in his memoirs thus: 'accounts of the brilliant success of the inauguration of a new Museum in the midst of one of the most crowded of the artisan districts of London appeared in the newspapers of the 25th June, 1872'.[7] There is no doubt that he was not alone in reading the event in this optimistic way. However the opening of the museum also revealed the precariousness of England's optimism and for all shades of opinion the physical reminders that the population of the East 'is either struggling on the brink of pauperism or has just dipped under' may well have echoed the thought circulated by Matthew Arnold three years earlier in *Culture and Anarchy* that one in twenty of the new national 'us' was a pauper. Sweetness and light was perhaps as far away from Bethnal Green in June 1872 as a silver-gilt candelabra was from a tin tray decorated with tin-foil letters.

NOTES

1. This article forms part of a larger study of Bethnal Green, which includes a fuller analysis of the museum.

2. The article is based on a number of accounts of the Museum's opening ceremony and earliest days published between 25 June and 6 July 1872. The chief newspaper sources are: The *Times, Daily Telegraph, Daily News, Illustrated London News, Metropolitan, Architect, Echo*. The journal sources are: *The People's Magazine* 1 April 1873, The *Saturday Review* vol. 33, no.870, June 1872, and *Atlantic Monthly*, January 1873, the latter written by Henry James.

3. The idea of workmen as the country's new 'masters' surfaces in several places in the late 1860s. For example, John Morley in his *Life of Gladstone*: 'After the extension of the franchise to the working man, everyone felt, in a happy phrase of that time that "we must educate our masters".'

4. Physick, J (1988), *The Victoria and Albert Museum and the history of its building*, London 1982, p.146 notes that the railings were 'torn down in 1866 during a demonstration'. The contemporary quote in this paragraph is from the *Metropolitan*, 4 May 1872 which does not mention 1866 specifically.

5. Anon (1872) *A guide to the Bethnal Green branch of the South Kensington Museum*, Spotiswoode, London, contains the fullest account of the museum's first displays.

6. Correspondence between the Science and Art Department and the Treasury contained in ED. 84/244 (public records held at the National Archive of Art and Design) contains more detail about the various justifications of State funding for the museum.

7. Cole, H (1884). *Fifty Years of Public Work of Sir Henry Cole*, London, Volume 1 p.354.

A date with destiny

Greenwich and the millennium celebrations

Liz Greenhalgh

I think that the Festival (of Britain) had a real and lasting effect on private life in Britain. Clothes, streets, houses and thousands of things in daily use have slowly got brighter and lighter ever since, and this change can be traced directly back. But paralleled to it has grown another change, a mental sluggish gloom, a love of crises and despondency. Doing a successful thing again usually goes flop, so another Festival of Britain, centred on London, would be to invite failure; but we do need a new celebration to wake us up again – perhaps a Carnival for Devolution? (Barbara Jones, designer for the Festival of Britain, writing in 1976.)[1]

The time

Crossing the threshold between the second to the third millennium, whether considered in religious terms or not, is inescapably momentous. If coming to terms with a 1000 year time-frame is too much, then there is always the more manageable step or bridge (aided by the hands of chivalrous politicians) to the twenty-first century. This time-frame is derived originally from a Christian world view, and other religions keep alive different configurations of calendars, of years, and weekly holy days. But now it is a secular date. For many, the idea of marking the millennium in religious terms - 2000 years since the 'birth of our Lord' is a an arbitrary relic. Indeed postmodern analysis would argue that historical time is a made up narrative and the idea of 'history' as we understand it has only existed since the Renaissance (Deeds Ernarth, 1992).

Nevertheless the current time-system, and therefore the millennium, is recognised, not only in the so-called Christian world but also as the time-frame of the global economy and, in this sense, is real enough. The integration and interdependence of nations is reliant on this harmonisation of time, held in place by computer networks. Hence, the recent alarm over the potential chaos and disruption that might be caused by computer systems unable to recognise the year 2000.

The right to party

If we regularly celebrate New Year's Eve, then why not celebrate with greater energy the end of the century, the end of the millennium and look forward, if not to the next 1000 years then the next century, or even just the next decade? We are obliged, according to common secular practice and custom and as The Artist Formerly Known As Prince exhorted, 'party like it's 1999'.

Given the past invention of British secular state festivals in 1851 and 1951, or spectacles and pageants like the Olympic festivals, it is not surprising that any government might suggest a popular national celebration, party or event to mark this historic passing of time, especially with the use of 'the people's money', the unexpected surplus millions generated by the National Lottery.

The place

Whilst every country has a millennium, not every country has the origin of zero longitude. If there was to be a celebration based on the theme of time, it would have to be in historic Greenwich. However compelling, efficient and well planned any other schemes were, the competition to stage the millennium celebrations, based as it is on the theme of time, was erroneous. Nowhere else in the country had the advantage of the meridian line and the brand of Greenwich mean time (GMT). The British Parliament has a direct link with the establishment of longitude at Greenwich. As Dava Sobel describes in her book *Longitude*, it was the British Parliament in 1714 that set up the Longitude Act, a competition with a large money prize for anyone who could come up with a 'Practicable and Useful' means of determining longitude (Sobel 1996).

Not far from the Observatory lies the peninsula, a 181 acre derelict riverside site, mostly closed off to the public and much of the land contaminated by the huge British Gas site operating there until quite recently. The land covers a huge and important river frontage of the Thames, but is currently closed and unused. On the face of it, reclaiming such an area of previously derelict land is uncontentious, its redevelopment has little negative impact, it does not involve uprooting and re-housing large numbers of people. Greenwich Council has been working for years on ideas and schemes to open up the peninsula as part of a wider strategy for making greater use of the River Thames. In 1989, Greenwich Council were exploring possibilities for using the 'time concept' and creating an exhibition or museum park. They were looking at ideas such as self-build plots or 'research and development living zones' as experiments in creating new urban settlements. They were concerned with making sure the public transport infrastructure was secure and that options for river transport were at least considered. In 1989 the Council realised they had one of the 'biggest brand names in the world' and that 'historic' Greenwich was then and still is one of the top tourist attractions in the country. (Comedia 1989).

The event

In some ways the idea of a celebration of the passing of the millennium has been overwhelmed by the arbitrariness of time and date. These factors are over-determining. The portentousness of time and date seem to outweigh the mere content of the event - whatever it is. How is it possible to sum up 1000 years of history and to anticipate the next 1000 years? Would it ever have been possible to think of what to do and why, before deciding that what ever it was, it had to happen? Maybe not. What is important is that something happens. And yet, the process leading to the decision to hold a festival at Greenwich has been dogged by uncertainty. The date was no secret. The opportunity was clear, it had been talked about for years, but exactly what it should be, was anything but. Various government ministers debated it in different guises. The difficulty was in moving from a vague and generalised idea to a clear plan of action.

The process of agreeing to hold the event was tortuous. The competition between Greenwich and Birmingham to stage the event was dragged out. The inevitability of London winning out yet again left a bad taste. Statements of private sector sponsorship commitment had to be forcibly extracted from London companies. Partnership teams broke up and re-assembled on opposing sides. The Labour Party refused to sign a blank cheque before it was in government. Deep reservations within the new Labour Cabinet were clear. The press was largely opposed. The final decision was taken only in June this year with two-and-a-half half years to go.

A conspiracy of silence

Uncertainty led to the effective gagging of everybody involved. Debate was stifled. Until the main objective of securing the project was achieved nobody could rock the boat. There was much public debate to be had - what would the legacy of the project be, what would the theme of the exhibition be, what kinds of choices could be taken within the framework for the project. Instead, the only public face of the project was the (unfair) competition between London and Birmingham. As time went by options were closing down. There was no point in having a discussion if the exhibition didn't happen. The whole project seemed to be sleepwalking into a strait-jacket; moving towards an exhibition of what is achievable given the limitations rather than what is desirable as an expression of greater aspiration.

The public consultation held in 1996, with its accompanying video loop and theme tune, showed maps, plans, architectural drawings and a model of the dome - but almost nothing of the content. It was described as a day visit which would attract 12 million people. A hive with no honey - why would we go? Journalists and TV researchers looking for the story couldn't find one. 'Not much open discussion' was a difficult peg to hang a story on. It seemed an idea without a clear purpose, a building without a function, a temporary project with an expensive price tag. And yet if the dome fell, the last few years effort would be wasted and alternatives and re-thinks would have to be started double quick. Either way it was a risk. Ironically the biggest problem left, is time.

A gap opened up between those close to power and therefore with some stake in the project, and an alienated or indifferent public. The would-be visionaries believed that the millennium had to be marked, that an exciting and forward looking exhibition was important, that the long-term potential for London was significant and that over the next two years, the momentum would build. In the meantime, bold, expensive and sometimes sweeping decisions had to be taken. The dissenters were put off by the huge sums involved, the wall of secrecy, the apparent self-aggrandisement of a few architect-kings and the fierce unrelenting commitment to the dome itself, the only tangible symbol of the whole project, its main asset being its enormous size - the largest covered structure in the world. The media coverage has continued to be overwhelmingly hostile, relentlessly portraying a project apparently lurching from crisis to crisis.

Back to the future

The Millennium Experience clearly sees itself as a direct successor to the Great Exhibition of 1851 and to the 1951 Festival of Britain. Such comparisons are inevitable. Both were defining moments in setting a public mood, image and national identity. They both had (however debatable) significant cultural legacies. 1851 led to the establishment of grand national museums in London and 1951 set the tone for post-war state support for the arts. However, it is not just these two events that have set precedents. The last 50 years has seen a huge amount of festivalisation as part of national and corporate expression. National exhibition centres have sprung up world-wide as cities have staged innumerable events as part of stadia regeneration. The link has been made between urban regeneration and the building of exhibition centres, or staging and hosting world-wide events from Olympic bids to World Student Games, Common Wealth Games, Expo sites and new sports stadia. Nearly every major city in Europe has some form of exhibition/ convention/sports centre. Recent decades have seen investment in G-Mex in Manchester, the ICC in Birmingham and the Olympic-standard sports facilities in Sheffield. Stadia-led regeneration with festivals, expos, conventions, trade-fairs and conference facilities were part of the essential repertoire of facilities in the modern service-centre city. The baton of the pleasure garden with funfairs, (famous in Battersea Park during the 1951 exhibition and after), passed to the private sector who took the idea and developed the commercial theme park often combining, as in the case of Jorvik, pure entertainment with 'educational' or historical themes.

There will be, it seems, a direct echo of architectural design from the 1950s to the year 2000 in the symbol of the dome design. The centrepiece for 1951 was the 'Dome of Discovery', described together with the skylon in a special edition of the *Illustrated London News* as 'part of a scene of remarkable architectural beauty in the modern manner' (Feaver 1951). Many argue that the South Bank Festival fixed the popularly accepted idea of modern for a whole generation and that architectural and design motifs influenced both the design of public architecture in the 1950s and 60s New Towns in Britain, and people's personal taste for design. It was the moment to chuck out the chintz.

If a British sense of the modern was crystallised in the 1950s, with its decisive link to the anticipation of space travel, spaceship design and images of flying-saucers, it seems to have stuck there, for it is striking just how reminiscent the Richard Roger Partnership design is of these 1950s modernist motifs. As with current car design, the contemporary design aesthetic is a retro-modernist look a coming to life of the comic cartoons of the 1950s turned into mass-produced nostalgia for the 1990s. The question of what is modern about dome design is left hanging and leads to a further question of whether architectural modernism's link between form, material and function has finally been broken. Is the dome a post-modern fantasy land where Tony Blair can shake hands with the Beatles?

The people's cultural policy

Following the 1948 'Britain can make it' exhibition, designed to promote British manufacturing, the 1951 Festival attempted to accelerate innovation in British design and architecture. An explicit attempt was made to recruit young designers and architects. The temporary nature of the exhibition and the structures within it allowed for experimentation in architecture, painting and design of the public spaces on the site. The exhibition organisers brought together a wide group of young designers, architects and painters. The director of science and technology for the 1951 exhibition drew on the advice and expertise of specialist panels of 150 top scientists representing all the branches of science. The Festival made an explicit attempt to bring together British innovation and achievements (Banham 1951).

The organisation of the 1951 festival reflected the position of the professional groups and the status of cultural institutions. The leading figures supporting and promoting the Festival of Britain were described as the radical middle-classes, the do-gooders, and the backbone of the BBC (Frayn 1963). The intention in 1951 was to use the existing national bodies, the Arts Council, the British Film Institute, the Council for Industrial Design and others. Special Councils were created for science and for architecture. (As it turned out the provision of thematic material and the briefing of designers was mainly done by the CoID and the Science Council, but the Arts Council commissioned a number of works of art specifically for the festival.) What is striking now is how little involvement the existing cultural establishment, the public professionals of the arts and other public 'councils' appear to have had in the plans for the celebrations in 2000. The appointment of the advertising and image consultants to define the content, the experience, the collective aspirations of a nation is perhaps one of the clearest statements we have had of the new group of cultural intermediaries in Britain.

The 1951 festival confirmed the role of public patronage and culture as a matter of state policy. This role is clearly changing. The old establishment of public culture (establishing its credibility in the 1950s) is being sidelined by the emergence of a different group of quangos, taskforces, consultancies and entrepreneurs financed by the new source of public finance, the Lottery. Presumably it will be new agencies that will run the Millennium Challenge Fund and Nesta - a National Endowment for Science, Technology and the Arts. The Creative Industries Taskforce is made up of young (ish) entrepreneurs in the worlds of music, fashion and film, the pioneers of Britain's creative economy.

It is not the ex-Directors of the Royal Opera House or the Arts Council that are brought in to help deliver the Greenwich project on time, but the ex-Sky TV executive. Is this new layer of entrepreneurial management to co-exist with past bureaucracies or are we witnessing a decisive shift in cultural policy?

The decision to stage the exhibition chimes with much that new Labour is trying to achieve in the re-branding of Britain. The Arts Council's role may well be limited as newer agencies are concerned with the convergence between arts and technology and the interactivity between production and consumption. These ideas underpin new Labour led aspirations of Britain as a 'creative nation' with a 'creative economy' built upon links between culture and communications.

Grounds for success

Unless a disaster happens between now and 1999, the Millennium Experience is likely to be a success, but in what terms - The 1951 Festival attracted 8.5 million visitors in 5 months. The Millennium Experience expects 12 million visitors in 12 months. If it reaches its target figures will that be enough? Setting the terms of success must be part of the thinking from now on. The worst-case scenario for the 'experience' is that people come, pay their entrance fee, have a mildly enjoyable experience and then go home and forget about it. The best-case scenario is for people to feel inspired to experience not just enjoyment, but creative insight about how individual life-chances can change, how the way we lead our lives will change, where the world is heading and what the possibilities are. It should aim to accelerate our thinking and generate breakthroughs. The legacy of the exhibition is as important as the event itself. Perhaps the most important realisation is that this cannot be delivered through the medium of a spectacle in an isolated container on the South Bank. To succeed, the idea of celebration has to have a life and a spirit that lives beyond the site itself and the symbol of the dome. This could happen in many different, and as yet, unpredictable ways. Reyner Banham argues that one of the most enduring, influential but undervalued and perhaps unexpected legacies of the 1951 festival was the innovation in urban design and the creation of the public spaces which were an integral part of the whole experience: not just visually with design and sensually with flowers and plants; but as the places where people walked, sat, danced and posed for photographs (Banham 1951). The philosophy of treating exterior spaces as equally important as the enclosed buildings created a legacy of urban design that has since been felt in every British city.

REFERENCES

Banham, M. and Hillier, B. (eds), (1951) *A Tonic to the Nation: The Fesival of Britain 1951*, London: Thames & Hudson.

Cox, I., quoted in *ibid*.

Deedes Emarth, E., (1992) *Sequel to History: Postmodernism and the Crisis of Representational Time*, Princeton, New Jersey: Princeton University Press.

Feaver, W., quoted in Banham (1951).

Frayn, M., (1963) *Festival in the Age of Austerity* in M. Sissons and P. French (eds) quoted in Banham *et al* (1951.

Sobel D., (1996) *Longitude*, London: Fourth Estate.

Comedia, (1989) *Greenwich 2001: a concept study*, London.

NOTES

1. See Banham, M. and Hillier, B. (eds), (1951) *A Tonic to the Nation: The Fesival of Britain 1951*, London: Thames & Hudson.

REVIEWS

Identity made, and not given

'Lara' reviewed

Bernardine Evaristo, *Lara*, Angela Royal Publishing, Tunbridge Wells 1997.

Nana Yaa Mensah

> It is of course true that the African identity is still in the making. There isn't a final identity that is African. But, at the same time, there *is* an identity coming into existence.
>
> Chinua Achebe

> ... I longed for an image,
> a story, to speak me, describe me,
> birth me whole.
> Living in my skin, I was, but which one?
>
> *Lara*, p69

Lara, Bernardine Evaristo's first novel, is but the latest installment of an ongoing exploration. What really makes up the mesh, asks this author, of the lives of people who claim more than one culture? In lyrical tones, Evaristo depicts the difficult business of the way in which an individual - in this case, a specially gifted child - goes about constructing an identity for herself.

Lara, fourth-born and spiritually blessed daughter in a family of eight, is the child of the Abbey Wood-born Ellen and the Lagosian Taiwo. Her mother comes of a line that has clawed its way from origins in the Irish famine up the social ladder and into the 'respectability' of a hardworking life in the south-east London suburbs. Taiwo is the descendant of freed Brazilian returnee slaves to the west coast of Africa. The young man is the classic case of the colonial subject who travels to England in the aftermath of the war, seeking to work, study further and make a fortune.

> ... A clarion call bugled
> the colonies and to a city burnt out from doodlebug
> and Luftwaffe, they doffed cap, donned greatcoat,
> dreams of prosperity, milk and gold, they were sold.
> Now the emperor's disowned sons
> congregate in Commonwealth dance halls. (p6)

It is here, in the half-lit land of free association and escapism, that Taiwo meets Ellen who, he immediately decides, will be the mother of his children.

The coming together of the races in this young family is symbolised by the huge rambling house near Woolwich Common into which they move soon after Lara's birth in Eltham. With Ellen producing a child virtually every year, the da Costas need the space.

> Atlantico sits like a fat Victorian dolls' house on its own high land ...
> on the bend of long Arundel Road which ambles towards the bleak wasteland of Woolwich Common. ...
> Its garden slopes like an untended terraced field citizened by two of apple, pear, and sweet and sour cherry trees,
> a wood lurks at the bottom, home to foxes and owls. ...
> An alley skulks down the garden's exposed right side;
> a garage, plastered to Atlantico's torso, is an artificial limb;
> huge Catholic windows stand watch over the distant Thames ...
> Sprawling, bedraggled, it is a wild mix of town and country. (p46)

The house lies in the shadow of the Catholic convent, in awe of its devoted postulants. It is this same church, however, which condemns her when she announces to her mother, Edith, her intention to marry a black man.

> ... Father Augustus ... said
> that taking the word of the Lord to the primitives is one thing, but it's quite another lying down with them. (p38)

Ellen has committed to a future with Taiwo, in the belief that their interracial love will conquer all. To the world of 1950s suburban London, however, this union symbolises the coming together of utterly incompatible opposites; the values of town (personified to the English by Ellen) meet those of Taiwo's 'untamed' nature - indeed, the 'bestiality' of all things black and unbridled.

It is out of this meeting and coalescing of 'town' and 'country' - through empathy, through a parallel history and through sex - that Lara is born in 1962. And it is at the meeting point of the threads of different influences, picking and choosing her coloured filaments with great care, that Lara must create for herself a web which shows off a sense of who exactly she is.

As a girl, our heroine sees visions of her Nigerian ancestors. Finally, however, Taiwo, tired of the child's 'mad' antics, beats her clairvoyant gifts out of her. Lara is no longer to see into the other world until the death of her English grandmother, who symbolises a form of European stranglehold over the young girl's imaginative life.

Yet here is a child cut off from both sides of her heritage. On her mother's side, grandmother Edith ('Nana') never quite manages to reconcile herself to the idea that her daughter has married a black man. Using a well-tried method, Edith blinds herself to the realities of the march of time. When her husband dies, Edith soldiers on, keeping up the spotless house in Abbey Wood that is a museum to the 1930s. The birth of her first grandchild however brings about a softening of her heart, particularly when she finds that the child is

> No thick-lipped negroid child, this, but a paler hybrid (p45)

Cut off as Edith is from the world of experience, for reasons of social ambition, the da Costa children will never gain more from their grandmother than an unthinking maternal love and 50 pence for trimming the lawn in summertime.

In such an environment, the children absorb some of the myths and prejudices of their elders and peers about the black races. Cousin Beatrice, on a visit from Liverpool in 1978, tries to impress on the young Lara a radicalised, politicised, equally constricting version of identity, inviting her to take sides.

> ... 'Lara, lovey, so long as you're of negroid stock, diluted or not, you're black, ask me how I know?'
> 'How d'ya know, Miss Africa?' 'The P word, prejudice.
> So it's about time you learnt some African ways, eh?
> I know the difference between yam and cassava. Do you?' (p76)

Taiwo, with the responsibility of a wife and eight children, finds it impossible to get ahead in English society. His duty to his offspring makes it imperative that he give them what he thinks will be the best start in life: forget about reading Shakespeare and Shelley for pleasure, forget his dreams of becoming a playwright, and hunker down to hard, badly paid work as a welder. His children are told nothing of their African history: after all, the key thing is that they learn that they belong in England and that they simply fit in.

Lara's efforts to question him meet with opaque responses. He remains gloriously vague on the subject of the 'home' culture and, most tellingly, on the matter of his Nigerian family.

> 'What was your mother like?' 'Oh very nice.' 'Yes but what was she like?' 'A very nice lady, I can safely say.' 'Well what was your father like?' 'He was very nice too.' (p81)

The first blow has already come in the form of a letter from his mother in Lagos, telling Taiwo of the death in childbirth of his twin sister Kehinde. When the children's Nigerian grandmother herself dies, Taiwo closes in on himself in grief, but cannot go home: there is no money, and anyway, he has not yet made his fortune. To return now, even for her burial, would be a matter of shame.

In this space dominated by silence and half-understood truths, the first-generation English-born da Costas flounder.

> Lara's skin oozed honey in late summer's oven ... Full on to the sun, its strokes painted her a rusty brown until sun-drunk, she stumbled inside.
> 'Look, I've got a sun tan!'
> 'Don't be silly, dear,' Ellen mumbled, rolling thick pastry.
> Three at a time, she vaulted the stairs, passing Fabian.
> 'Jagger-lips!' he teased, sliding down the bannisters, out of her reach.
> 'Watusi-head,' she retaliated loudly, reaching her attic bedroom and slamming the door. She studied her lips in the mirror, they weren't too big, not like her father's or that Nat King Cole man whose boring Mona Lisa drifted up the stairs at night. Still, she'd suck them in from now on, just in case. (p60)

At the same time, they are unable to participate fully in these 'home truths'.

> 'Where 'you from, La?' Susie suddenly asked one lunch break on the playing fields. 'Woolwich.'
> 'No, silly, where are you from, y'know, originally?'
> 'If you really must know I was born in Eltham, actually.'
> 'My dad says you must be from Jamaica,' Susie insisted.
> 'I'm not Jamaican! I'm English!'
> 'Then why are you coloured?'
> Lara's heart shuddered, she felt so humiliated, so angry.
> 'Look, my father's Nigerian, my mother's English, alright!'
> 'So you're half-caste!' Lara tore at the grass in silence.
> 'Where's Nigeria then, is it near Jamaica?' 'It's in Africa.'
> 'Where's Africa exactly?' 'How should I know, I don't bloody well live there, do I!' 'Is your dad from the jungle?' (p65)

It is ironic that it is out of this unpromising suburban scenario that Lara begins to discover who she is. The setting's tensions and the confining boxes into which it forces its inhabitants are precisely the catalyst for Lara to begin to question the world. She starts by working out what she does *not* want to be. Her original desire to be all things white and to avoid all things African transmutes into a wariness.

> In the showers at school I began to notice my difference. ...
> I wanted to be invisible. I wanted to be noticed. (p70)

Much later, she feels an all-consuming desire to journey to the land of her black forebears. Here, Lara begins to feel, she must surely discover the key part of her imaginative drive.

> When Nana died the sea began to

surge ... The sea would not leave me, though it wailed.
Lucky ... lu ... cki ... la ... ki ... Warmth enveloped me like an electric blanket, I felt buoyant, floating.
... Someone materialised in my room, like darkroom paper in developer, an image formed, a woman, I thought, dark-skinned, tall, I was not sure for it quickly faded out into murkiness, then air, but the music, the wind, the tune, encircled me.
'Bring him home,' it sang, 'Bring him home.' (p101)

It is fine art that is Lara's first stop in her quest to find out what inhabits the landscape of her imagination. But it is not art *per se* that plays the role of medium for translating her desire for greater self-discovery: the new places and people she discovers in London - Notting Hill, south London, the Chelsea, Chiswick and Fulham set at art college - convince her that she must seek herself further afield.

Portobello pub ... I hover in a dungeon alcove, nurse my port, insecure, wish I'd been born a Holland Park babe, was a funky half-caste dahling, a Cleo Laine jazztress with a voice that sails, seducing the crowd. (p91)

The filling in for her of the map of London runs parallel with the long-drawn-out falling into place of various pieces of a jigsaw puzzle that makes up her identity. Her yen to be black takes Lara into sexual adventure, in the form of a new boyfriend, the Eton-educated Nigerian Josh. Here, she fares no better and is no more at ease than with her West London friends.

'... you don't even know what Jollof rice is, let alone how to cook it. You're strictly a fish fingers and mash girl. You'll make a sorry wife.'
He sniffed, smugly sipped his drink, crossed his legs.
'Why don't you put me down, Bertie Wooster, you know for a change, and who says I only like Nigerian men?'
'It's obvious, you hope some of it will rub off on you.'
'Oh fuck off, you idiot! ...' (p90)

Lara's attempts to find out about her Brazilian/Nigerian culture have already met with resistance. Edith's reaction to her granddaughter's announcement that she would like to visit Nigeria has been simple:

... 'What do you want to go there for? You'll come back looking like a nigger-man, dear.' (p84)

But journey back Lara does, first with her parents, on a visit to Lagos. In the land of the father's and daughter's forebears, Taiwo wanders around in a daze as 'The past swamps him, like a drowning man' (p105). Through photographs, landmarks and shared stories, the now grown-up Lara gains her first sense of who these people were whose lives helped make hers possible. What has been largely a chronological narrative in verse, with precise situations in time along a linear historical trajectory, dissolves into something much more fluid. Through a photograph of her grandmother Zenobia, wife of the freed Brazilian slave Gregorio, Lara connects with 1935, simultaneously making a link with her childhood memories of the 'Daddy people', her ancestors who appeared to her in daylight visions.

The complex interweaving of histories and breaking down of finite distinctions of race in this one girl's history, in search of her culture, signal the coming of a new idea of what it means to be African. As Kwame Anthony Appiah (Appiah 1992) writes:

> ... a biologically rooted conception of race is both dangerous in practice and misleading in theory: African unity, African identity, need securer foundations than race.

Lara's exploration of self does not fit a strictly pan-Africanist mould: it follows rules which are necessarily super-racial, in order to arrive at a new sense of what it means to be African.

Next, she journeys to Brazil and to Bahia, birthplace of Lara's greatgrandfather. The historical continuum here begins in 1839, rupturing in 1875, when Baba takes his son Gregorio back to Yorubaland. The voyage wrenches the thirteen-year-old away from his mother Joana - a slavewoman who refuses to leave Bahia, 'my home' - but reconnects him with the homeland of his ancestors: the pull of *candomblé* and the *orixas*.

This Afro-Brazilian dimension to Lara's reconstruction of her past recalls a recent talk given in London by John Picton, Reader in the History of African Art at the School of Oriental and African Studies. At a conference marking the opening of the exhibition 'Rhapsodies in Black', a celebration of the Harlem Renaissance of the 1920s, Picton delivered a talk on the fabrication of identity. He selected as his context the creation of the idea of Yoruba identity at the end of the 19th century.

Choosing his references from the history of art education in Nigeria, Picton signalled the role of politics in creating the movement that led to the very coining of the term 'Yoruba'. The impetus to consolidate an indigenous culture, faced with the arrival in Lagos of *emancipados* from Brazil, on the one hand, and the presence of colonising forces, on the other, led a loose and disparate spread of peoples, Picton suggested, to gather under the banner of this new joint identity.[1]

It is a variant of this same

process that Lara, as the mixed-raced product of cultures that are in themselves mixed - Nigerian, Brazilian, Portuguese and Irish with English - must engage in as she works out what her space in the world will be. In this fine novel, using structures both subtle and keen, Lara finds that the choices offered by her more rigidly self-defined relations are entirely inadequate. And ultimately, she discovers that the space in which her identity will be able to breathe most freely must be located where this is geographically and spiritually possible, *after* her journey into the past. In sum, Lara is profoundly English, in a way that looks forward to the twenty-first century and a new age of self-invention:

> ... I will wing back to Nigeria again and again, excitedly swoop over a zig-zag of amber lights signalling the higgledy energy of Lagos.
>
> It is time to leave. Back to London, across international time zones,
> I step out of Heathrow and into my future. (p140)

REFERENCES

Appiah, K.A., (1992) *In My Father's House: Africa in the Philosophy of Culture* Oxford: Oxford University Press.

NOTES

1. K.A. Appiah also describes the consolidation of Hausa-Fulani, Yoruba and Igbo identity in Nigeria as 'a product of the rough-and-tumble of the transition through colonial to postcolonial status' (*In My Father's House*, p177). Identity is 'real', he signals, because we imbue it with meaning and believe in it.

Stanley Reed

Bringing film to the people

David Robinson

Stanley Reed, director of the British Film Institute between 1964 and 1972, was a man with a heroic commitment to education as well as to cinema. He was born on 21 January 1911 in Plaistow, and cherished memories of a boyhood spent exploring the streets of East London. His father was a printer and his mother had been in domestic service before her marriage. An uncle who was a cabinet maker gave him a love of craftsmanship: he remained an enthusiastic woodworker to the end of his life.

Reading, though, was his passion. He remembered as a boy borrowing a book from the local lending library, finishing it on the way home, and going back for another without even entering the house. He won a scholarship to Stratford Grammar School, which was co-educational, and where, at 11, he met and fell for Alicia Chapman, whom he was to marry fifteen years later. The school staff appealed vainly to Alicia for help in overcoming this able but insubordinate pupil's unwillingness to play games or wear his school cap.

He went on to give no less anxiety to the conservative staff of the College of St Mark and St John, Chelsea, where he studied for English honours and a teaching certificate, and where his enterprise in forming a students' union, as well as dramatic and orchestral societies was seen as dangerously radical.

In 1932 he returned to the East End to teach senior elementary pupils at Credon Road Boys School. Startlingly ahead of his time, he introduced film studies into his English classes. As a boy he had made pinhole cameras and he remained fascinated by photography. Now he began to experiment with amateur films. Together with Alicia he was active in the organisation of the pioneer West Essex Film Society, and the couple seized every opportunity that London offered for seeing foreign films.

After the war, during which he was kept busy with the school's evacuation programme, Reed returned to West Ham as Visual Aids Officer of the Education Committee. He also collaborated on a film about the borough's restoration programme, Neighbourhood 15, which he wrote and narrated. (It reappeared on television last year in a BBC programme about the subsequent development of the renamed Newham). Reed's active involvement in the campaign to save Wanstead Flats from development threatened to jeopardise his career with the Council however, and he gratefully accepted the newly created post of Education Officer at the British Film Institute.

He had found his ideal niche in what was then a small organisation manned by like-minded film enthusiasts. He was now able to extend the pioneer work of promoting the understanding and appreciation of film, begun in the schools of West Ham on a national scale. He lectured tirelessly around the country, making 'film appreciation' a recognised school discipline. A brilliant communicator, he could thrill school children with the physical quality of a strip of film, as well as inspiring them with the images on the screen.

In 1956 Reed became secretary of the British Film Institute, and in 1964 succeeded James Quinn as its director. As secretary he could seem rigid and authoritarian: he would cut off opposition with a sharp and definitive 'I don't accept that'. His period as director however brought out the best in himself and in the organisation. He was brave and visionary and found a valuable ally in Labour's Arts Minister Jenny Lee. In his eight years at the BFI the staff grew dramatically, but without ever prejudicing the founding aims of the BFI, of promoting the art and understanding of film, or succumbing to the inappropriate corporate ambitions which were later increasingly to impair the Institute's functioning.

Among the activities that flourished notably under Reed's administration was the BFI's Production Board: headed by Mamoun Hassan, the Board's triumphs at this time included the first works of Bill Douglas and Mike Leigh. Reed was also concerned with the regional expansion of the BFI's work, and after his retirement in 1972 served for four years as consultant, helping to set up an effective organisation of regional film theatres.

After the British Film Institute, Reed embarked on a characteristically energetic retirement in the East London that he had never left or ceased to love. He remade his garden, to which he generally devoted each morning, while in the afternoon he set out with his camera, on foot or by bus, to photograph London suburbia. The other moments he filled with carpentry, watching films on television, listening to opera, and, of course, reading.

Stanley Reed, who resolutely refused all official honours, though he was happy to secure them for his BFI staff, is survived by his widow and their three daughters.

Stanley William Reed, cineaste, born Plaistow, London, 21 January 1911; died 4 May 1996, Wanstead, London.

This first appeared in the Guardian *and is reproduced with thanks.*